Weather in the City

Sanda Lenzholzer

Weather in the City

How Design Shapes the Urban Climate

nai010 publishers

Table of Contents

Foreword

A city can be mapped. A map to find your way is a different map than one to study morphology, and a cadastral map is again different from that. You can also see the city in a wholly new light. Forget the space for a moment and try to 'read' the city as an organism in which a large number of complex processes from our industrial society come together. An organism, moreover, streams flow into, to be processed or influenced and then flow out again, in short: an organism showing all the signs of metabolism. The various processes and streams (energy, food, data, cargo, biota et cetera) of this metabolism highly determine the functioning of the city. And all of them are, from a designer's perspective, worthy of closer inspection.

Of all streams touching the city, air isn't the most tangible. It is invisible, yet can be felt. It can touch you and when the wind plays with your hair, it can momentarily connect you to something bigger, to the outside world, to the clouds you see drifting in the sky. Every city writes the choreography for an everlasting air-ballet. An ever-changing dance of air movements, all part of what you might call the urban micro-meteorology. The stony city becomes warmer than its surroundings, in extreme cases even by ten degrees. Highway mirages are the icon of *Summer in the City*. The warm city air rises, and the lower air pressure this causes is balanced by the surrounding – hopefully cool – air being sucked in. The topography and shape of a city largely determine the temperature differences between the city and its surroundings. In turn, the proximity and character of these surroundings – Are they green? Is there water? – determine if the air sucked into the city will offer its inhabitants some cooling.

'Large' meteorology works exactly the same way. Air movements between high and low pressure areas produce winds of different speeds, from no more than a whisper to raging storms. The layout of the city directs, transforms or blocks these air movements. The city sometimes adds to the sounds of the wind. The deflected, locally blocked and sometimes sped up air can literally howl, roar and whistle in the city. The wind sweeps through the streets and shakes the treetops. The urban choreography not only determines how the air moves, but also what is allowed to dance in the air. The urban functioning, the urban metabolism intentionally or unintentionally adds all kinds of substances and other gasses to the passing air. The vapour of cooling installations, the exhaust fumes of cars, the emissions of factories, the carbon dioxide emissions of power stations, the fine dust of all these activities, and smells, numerous smells. Just like water, the air is a medium you can add, mix or dilute all kinds of things in; but not unlimitedly, not without consequence. City air is liberating, but you have to be able to breathe.

In one city, the choreography steers toward a wild, modern ballet in which people are blown off their bicycles when the wind comes from the wrong direction, or a toxic ecology of smog is brewed that is literally breath-taking. Other cities come across as sheltered places or are known for their fresh air, often a successful combination of topography and adequate environmental measures taken in the past.

That a city's topography, structure and layout write the choreography for the air-ballet opens the perspective that we can influence the dancing air and be co-writers of its score. For cannot use, structure and layout be influenced by the administrators, planners and designers of the city? Naturally, you could only determine the topography of a city if you were to design a New Town from scratch. Can cities be designed with wind and climate as the starting points? Of course they can! The history of urban development is full of beautiful cities and towns perfectly attuned to their situation and setting in the landscape. Think of fishermen's towns built in such a way that they offer shelter from storms from the prevailing wind directions.

Think of ancient China. The oldest document known to me, from the second century before Christ and relating a much older oral tradition, *The Rites of Zhou*, provides precise directions on how to build a city. A square consisting of nine quadrants, dissected by nine north-south roads and nine east-west roads, with three gates in all four wind directions, the northern gates always to be closed. Ideally, mountains would protect the north side of city and a river or another water body could be found south of it. This way, an ideal configuration could be achieved for the Chi (energy) to flow optimally through the city, providing its citizens with wealth and prosperity. You can read references to the later Feng Shui into it and the important role of numerology is clear – each scale prominently features the square and the number nine – but these directions also had practical back-grounds, about the optimal layout of a city based on natural and landscape givens, in other words: considerations of what we would now call the 'urban climate'. I always have to take a moment to let it sink in that at the time the Batavians in Europe hollowed out tree trunks to float down the river Rhine, there was already a guidebook to building cities in China, which, by the way, also covered geography and agriculture, and (indeed) the spatial planning of the entire empire.

For a long time, we have neglected to integrate climate issues in our urban design. Once in a while, scale models of new city districts do get tested in wind tunnels, but this is not standard procedure. More often, it is done afterwards to diagnose and correct failings and problems, for instance when it turns out a building produces the most awful whistles. Also when it comes to heat, we will sooner see scientists monitoring large urban areas than active attention being given to possible mitigating measures in the design. In short: we can do tests afterwards, but it is no longer mostly in the mind of the designer.

We can't keep ignoring the urban climate. The size of our cities and vast urban landscapes create urban heat island effects, which can make it almost impossible to live in a city or parts of it in the summer, and which can be dangerous to vulnerable groups such as the elderly or children. This is a relative problem in our temperate climates, but more to the south and especially in the tropics, the urban heat island effect is literally a killer. Climate change in combination with unbridled urban expansion adds another dimension to the problem. That it wouldn't be that bad in our cities is no reason to ignore the urban climate. Not only can the city be a much more comfortable place to be, but a well-designed living environment can also be the difference between having to place air conditioning everywhere or not, which doesn't only devour energy, but also solves the indoor climate problem by exporting it to the outside environment, blowing out all that heated air.

This book is about reviving designs with a focus on on the urban climate. About examples of how to do this adequately. About the instruments we have at our disposal. The ancient Chinese weren't far off where this is concerned. Feng Shui literally means 'wind' and 'water', and those are also the main elements for optimizing the urban climate. You can steer the wind by optimizing the urban layout and by modelling the shape of buildings, the dimension of squares and the profiles of streets: the shape of the public space. You can cool the warm city air through strategic placement of open areas. In the city or outside of it.

In this day and age, when everything has to be legitimized through cost-benefit analyses, we can say that we are only two handshakes apart from hard, economic advantages. A good urban climate adds to the high scores of cities like Vancouver,

Copenhagen and Zürich in the charts for best cities in the world. In conclusion: if we manage to write such a choreography for the air-ballet that the resulting urban climate produces a comfortable living climate, we will be rewarded with a thriving business and living climate.

Prof. Dirk Sijmons

Acknowledgements

For me, writing this book was an important part of my mission to raise awareness of the urban climate. I noticed that only very few people working in all these fields 'creating' the city, knew about the urban climate. But I also noticed that many colleagues and students were very interested in this topic, as I was invited to be a guest lecturer at many firms, governmental institutions, universities, universities of applied sciences and conferences. A long time ago, I also started teaching practical modules to my students and giving workshops/master classes for professionals, in which we design for the urban climate. Designing with the urban climate in mind really inspired the participating colleagues and students, and they saw it as a supplement to their design repertoire. I would like to thank all these people for their enthusiasm and their encouragement to write this book!

I am very grateful to a number of people and organizations enabling me to make this book. First of all, I would like to express my gratitude to all financial contributors: Wageningen University and Stichting NHBOS and those who financed the Dutch version of this book.

Adrie van 't Veer and Monique Jansen, thank you so much for helping me prepare the layout and the graphs; and my graduate student Irina Hotkevica thank you for the shadow simulations. I am also very grateful to my colleagues for their feedback on the manuscripts: Garmt Arbouw and Jan Elsinga (Ministry of Infrastructure and the Environment), Hans van Ammers and Anneke Belksma (municipality of Arnhem), Monique Jansen and Bert van Hove (Wageningen University) and Cor Jacobs (Alterra).

Introduction:
Why this Book?

Have you ever been unable to fall asleep on a sweltering summer night – even though your windows were wide open? Has the wind ever almost swept you up on a city square? Or have you ever been blown off your bicycle at the foot of a tall building? This last thing happened to me when I had just moved to a coastal city in the Netherlands. I remember being very surprised; as I did not know wind could be *that* strong. But I did not yet connect it to the phenomena of the weather in the city, or, in technical terms: the urban climate. The heat and strong winds at specific spots are typical phenomena of the urban climate and we all feel it, be it usually unconsciously.

We all experience the urban climate

Unfortunately, many of the people involved in the design of cities lacked a more 'active' awareness of the urban climate. I used to be one of those people. When I was working as an urban designer, for instance, I once designed a beautiful, open square, which was constructed precisely as planned. However, after just one 'outdoor' season, people started complaining about wind nuisance. Regrettably, the clients, who knew the location very well, and I had not considered the issue of the urban climate. In the end I had to design matching windscreens for the square, but this solution 'with hindsight' interfered with the open concept of the original design. Had we all thought about the urban climate from the start, none of this would have happened!

These experiences pointed me to the urban climate theme and with time I deepened my knowledge of this subject, especially in my research on how people experience the microclimate in squares. I soon found out that there was a lot of scientific knowledge about the urban climate. I also noticed that people know surprisingly much about the microclimate (through direct, daily experience). My research showed that the way people experience the microclimate is not only determined by physical factors such as temperature and wind, but also by psychological factors such as ambiance. As my study progressed, I also came to

The urban climate is rarely a theme in urban design and policy

realize that those who 'make' the city paid far too little attention to the urban climate and that this significantly reduced the quality of life in cities. My research highlighted this problem, and the overwhelming attention it got from the media (regional and national television, radio, newspapers and websites) suggested that apparently I had hit a nerve. Three years later, when the first version of the book you hold in your hands came out in Dutch, the public and media attention was even larger, a clear sign that the urban climate theme deserves more attention. People liked how accessible this book was, with its clear language, visual communication and applicability. International colleagues from many different fields then asked me to publish an English version of this book as well, as it clearly meets a demand. This book, in English and adapted for an international readership, is the result.

Urban climate is not the same as the climate in the countryside

The lack of awareness of the urban climate among many of the 'makers' of cities became clear by their neglect of the fact that cities have their own specific climates. Despite clear scientific proof of the existence of the phenomenon urban climate, I still regularly see that designers and policy-makers ignore this fact. We have known for quite some time that the urban climate has a number of characteristics clearly distinguishing it from the climate of the surrounding landscapes. Due to the impact of buildings and streets, the air temperature in cities is at least 1 °C higher; usually the difference is even bigger, up to 10 °C at night. This impact also causes the air in cities to have up to 10 per cent lower relative humidity and 30-50 per cent lower wind speeds, and much stronger winds at specific spots. The built environment clearly is of great influence on our cities' climates. In many countries, however, there is still little awareness of the fact that every intervention in the urban tissue is in fact an intervention in the urban climate; and that the urban climate is thus largely 'designed' by those who make the city.

Climate change makes urban climate problems worse

The urban climate is of course also affected by global climate change. Generally speaking, there is a clear rise in temperature, and in almost all countries on earth the predicted effect of climate change in the near future is that their climates will be warmer. In the Netherlands, for example, the temperature has risen with 1.7 °C since 1900. That does not seem like much, but such an increase has an enormous impact on all natural processes and on the human body's temperature management. The International Panel for Climate Change (IPCC) is one of many to recognize this trend of global warming. It has made climate change scenarios for possible future situations. There are different outcomes for different countries, and some countries translate these scenarios to their national circumstances. In some countries, the rise in temperature will lead to more droughts, whereas other countries can expect more precipitation and downpours, and sometimes changing wind patterns as well.

The most important influence of climate change on the urban climate is its impact on urban temperature regimes. With temperatures rising in general, the temperatures within cities will rise as well. Global warming thus adds to the urban heat island effects. Heat waves can then become a much bigger problem for those who live in cities. These predicted effects will negatively affect people's health and productivity, and mortality rates are expected to go up. To prevent these heat-related problems, we need to act soon and adapt to these effects in urban planning. When wind patterns are expected to change, cities can be adapted, but this will only be an issue in some countries. The changes in precipitation patterns also require small adjustments with regard to the experience of the microclimate: better protection against the rain in our cities' outdoor areas. Generally speaking, probably the greatest challenge climate change poses is addressing the urban heat problems of the future.

In time, another global change will influence the urban climate: the use of energy. The world's sources of fossil energy will be depleted and renewable, clean energy sources will have to take their place. Today, the use of fossil energy causes air pollution in many cities. This will no longer be such a problem when we use clean energy sources. The need to address air pollution issues in urban (re)design is thus getting smaller as well. Therefore, I have not incorporated the theme of air pollution in this book.

Renewable energy lessens air pollution

We need to prepare for climate change and its effects. Being the ones who design the city, we need to be aware of the consequences of our designs on the way people experience the microclimate. This experience is closely related to people's health, but also to the usability and liveability of cities. So it is very important for everyone involved in urban planning to know about microclimates and the urban climate. For large-scale interventions, policymakers and planners at city and regional government bodies should get to work. On smaller scales, (future) urban designers, landscape architects and designers of the urban interior and street furniture. It also concerns those who indirectly influence the design of the urban environment, such as managers, developers, and retail and gastronomy organizations, and city branders.

We need to start working on the urban climate

I have written this book to fill the knowledge gap about the way people experience the phenomena of urban climate and how to design for them, in what I hope is an accessible, visually appealing and structured way. For this book, I will translate

Aim and target group of this book

scientific knowledge into useful design knowledge, primarily meant for those working in temperate climate zones. Part of this knowledge comes from my own research into microclimate experiences. This book has been written for a broad public in accessible language. The differences in readers' background and knowledge might mean that some of the information shared in this book is already known to part of this broad public.

What this book is about

Knowledge about the urban climate and how it can be influenced through design concerns various scales ranging from small to large, as you can influence the urban climate on all these levels. But before we discuss the urban climate itself, we should clarify our perspective on it: how we humans perceive our microclimatic surroundings, in other words the concept of microclimate experience. This concept has three main aspects, which also determine the structure of this book: physical temperature experience, physical wind experience and psychological aspects of microclimate experience. The pages of this book are colour-coded according to these three aspects, for easy navigation: red for temperature, blue for wind and yellow for psychological aspects. After discussing how these factors determine people's experience of microclimates, they can be used to expound on the urban climate. The chapters about analysis and adaptation of the urban climate are similarly structured according to these three aspects. You should always analyse the climate before you start designing for the urban climate. Therefore, this book contains suitable analysis methods and design solutions for different scale levels. The analyses and solutions work differently on large scales than they do on small scales. Various planning and design instruments can be of influence: from regional structural planning to detailed plans. Chapters 3 and 4 concern the large scale of the entire city, whereas chapters 5 and 6 focus on the small scale, from neighbourhood to paving stone. For the micro level there are very many design solutions. To distinguish them according to the readers' typical work fields these are subdivided into five spatial types: the direct environment of buildings, gardens and parks, squares, streets and parking facilities. This book's structure with its focus on scale and space will be easy to use for everyone who 'makes' the city, thus facilitating the 'design of the urban climate'. The book also contains many illustrations to show how the urban climate works and especially how we can adapt it. I sincerely hope the examples appeal to the imagination of the cities' 'makers' and encourage them to adapt our cities with the urban climate in mind.

1

How We Experience the Microclimate

The microclimatic environment is vital to us human beings, because our physiology only functions well in a relatively small range of temperature and wind circumstances. The need to create a comfortable microclimate directly around our body determines for example what clothes we decide to wear and whether we stay indoors or go outside. When we are outside we usually opt for a certain microclimatic environment, even if we often do so unwittingly. Depending on our microclimatic need, we choose a sunny or shaded spot or route, in the wind or protected from it. The 'ambiance' also plays a role in our experience of the microclimate, so if we experience a place to be 'warm' or 'cold'. The microclimate experience helps us seek out places beneficial to our physiological and psychological well-being. We can think of these different aspects as pieces of a puzzle supplementing each other to complete the big picture of microclimate experience. Because urban design can influence this experience of the microclimate, we need to know which aspects we can influence through design and which ones we cannot.

The many factors influencing the way people experience the microclimate can be categorized in three clusters (see illustration 1). The first contains the individual physical and physiological factors, such as age, metabolism and clothing. These can't be influenced through urban design. The second cluster contains the external physical stimuli for people's sensation of temperature and wind (see illustration 2). A combination of factors has an effect on the temperature sensation. Air temperature and the influence of long and shortwave radiation determine it to a large extent (see section 2.1). Wind sensation is also very important for the physical microclimate experience. To a lesser extent, the microclimatic experience is influenced by the air's relative humidity. Especially the temperature and wind sensation can be influenced through design measures. Psychological factors form the third cluster. In part, these can be manipulated through the design of the city as well.

You can make calculations on the physical factors with a combination of 'thermal indices'. For indoor spaces, for example, an index based on air temperature and radiation is often used. More complex indices also take air movement, clothing, metabolism and such into account. To calculate the microclimate with these indices, you either need extensive measurements or computer simulations, and that is work for experts. Usually, however, you do not need to use these indices. Those designing for the urban climate should primarily keep the combination of thermal and wind sensation in mind and know that environmental psychological factors often also come into play. The size of the boxes with the influential factors in illustration 1 gives a rough outline of the interaction between these factors, and whether or not they can be influenced through design.

This chapter describes the different factors influencing microclimate experience one by one. First the physical factors air temperature, short- and longwave radiation, relative humidity and wind. The psychological factors are discussed next. Urban design can have an effect on all these factors. This chapter also features factors that can't be manipulated through design.

1.1 Physical Factors of Microclimate Experience

1.1.1 Experience of Temperature

The influence of air temperature

The first and best-known factor often chosen to express temperature sensation is the air temperature, even though more factors play a role, as we can see in illustration 2. On a scale of just a few metres, the air temperature in outdoor areas in cities only changes minimally. It does change during the day, with maximum temperatures in the afternoon and minimum temperatures at night (with few exceptions). Of course, air temperatures change with the seasons as well. Urban design interventions can have a limited effect on air

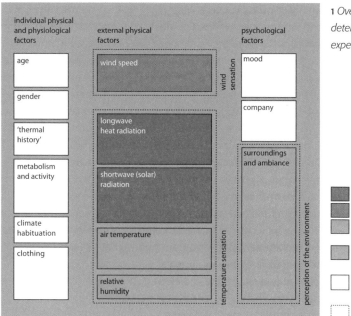

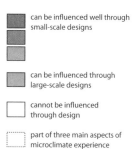

■ can be influenced well through small-scale designs

■

■

■ can be influenced through large-scale designs

□ cannot be influenced through design

┈ part of three main aspects of microclimate experience

temperatures on a small scale. Many small measures combined *do* have a great effect, for instance when a city is planted with many trees, decreasing air temperatures with their shade and evapotranspiration.

Another factor with a very strong influence on thermal experience is short- and longwave radiation (see section 2.1.1), which can give people a sense of warmth. How we feel short- and longwave radiation should not be confused with the way we experience air temperatures. The differences between these types of temperature experience can clearly be felt in a number of situations. A typical example of our experience of shortwave radiation can be felt outside, when we go from a sunny place with high levels of shortwave solar radiation into the shade. On a small scale of only a few metres, the air temperature between these two spots is not different. But as we all know, the direct radiation of the sun does make the sunny spot and the shaded one feel very different. We know the longwave radiation emitted by materials well, for instance when we sit in front of a warm wall in the evening after a very sunny day. Even though the air temperature has come down, our body is still kept warm by the wall's heat radiation. This example demonstrates another important aspect of this radiation: its orientation. We can clearly feel the direction the radiation is coming from and the parts of our body exposed to the radiation source are warmed as opposed to those that are not exposed. So heat radiation has a prominent effect on the way we experience temperatures and spatial measures can make a real difference.

The influence of shortwave solar radiation and longwave heat radiation

The influence of the relative humidity of the air

The relative humidity also has an influence on the way we experience temperatures. For example, a very high level of atmospheric humidity on a muggy day can have a negative effect on people's thermal comfort. The air is saturated with vapour and can't take up people's sweat. Just like air temperature, relative humidity is quite uniform on small scales, and can hardly be influenced by spatial measures.

Heat stress

Extreme heat conditions can significantly disturb people's thermoregulation and this can have serious consequences. This especially applies to the impact of heat, because heat is much harder to avoid or prevent than cold is, since people can put on warmer clothes when it's cold or stay indoors. For many people heat stress does not only make them feel uncomfortable, but also negatively affects their concentration and productivity. We are talking about a decrease in productivity of over 10 per cent here, a very costly phenomenon for society. Add to this the trouble people have sleeping on hot nights: it takes longer for them to fall asleep, and when they do their sleep is shorter and not as deep. For vulnerable groups such as children, elderly people, obese people, people suffering

2 *Physical factors influencing outdoor microclimate experience*

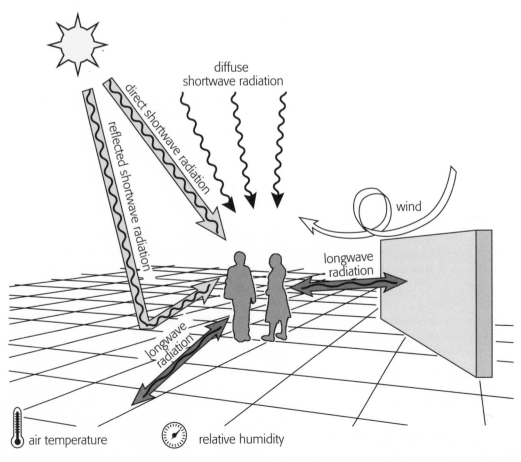

diffuse shortwave radiation

direct shortwave radiation

reflected shortwave radiation

wind

longwave radiation

longwave radiation

air temperature

relative humidity

from heart, lung or blood pressure conditions and for pregnant women, heat stress can cause various health problems. Think of heat rash, heat cramps, exhaustion, dehydration, kidney failure and breathing problems.

These issues are reflected in the number of people consulting their doctor about heat-related problems or even having to be hospitalized. The heat waves we've had in the last years resulted in significantly higher mortality rates. In the summer of 2003, for example, nearly 15,000 people died in France because of the heat (see illustration 4). A short heat wave lasting a couple of days generally leads to a higher mortality rate of 10 to 15 per cent in many countries.

Serious heat-related health risks and mortality

1.1.2　Experience of Wind

The movement of the air, for example draft or wind, is important for how people experience the microclimate as well. When the air moves, it absorbs more sweat and heat from the skin than it

Wind chill

Location	Date	Extra deaths	Increase (%)
England and Wales	August, 4th – 13th	2091	17
France	August, 1st – 20th	14802	60
Germany	August, 1st – 24th	1410	–
Italy	June 1st – August 15th	3134	15
The Netherlands	June – September	1400 - 2200	–
Portugal	August	1854	40
Spain	July – August	4151	11
Switzerland	June – September	975	7

4 *Higher mortality during the heat wave of 2003 in several European countries*

5 *How will these girls safely cross this windy square?*

does when it is still, providing the air temperature is lower than that of the skin, which is usually the case in temperate zones. The faster the air moves, the more heat and sweat it absorbs. That is why weather reports in some countries include *wind chill factor* forecasts apart from the temperature forecasts. The direction of the air movement is a factor as well. Body parts directly exposed to the wind cool faster than other parts do. But we do not only feel air movement as a decrease in temperature; we also feel its kinetic energy. There are different degrees of this type of wind effect.

We might be uncomfortable at wind speeds of 1 to 4 metres per second, with our hair blowing in the wind and our clothes fluttering. We speak of wind nuisance when speeds reach 4 to 15 metres per second, because these speeds make it harder to walk or ride a bicycle. Speeds over 15 metres per second are considered dangerous, even walking is very difficult in strong winds like these. Wind speeds over 20 metres per second will simply blow people over.

Wind nuisance

1.1.3   Other Physical Factors

A number of factors that play a role in people's thermoregulation are connected to the individual person and his or her activities and behaviour. The way people dress is the first thing that comes to mind. Everyone dresses according to their own ideas – whether these clothing choices are really appropriate for the weather conditions or not. Another main individual factor of microclimate experience is physical activity. When we exercise, our metabolism is boosted and we warm up faster than when we are at rest. A person's 'thermal history' also plays a role. When we step from a hot sauna into frosty air, for example, it will take us a few minutes to feel the cold. Gender and age are also big factors when it comes to individual microclimate experience. Women are more sensitive than men and older people are more sensitive than younger ones. Habituation is another factor. People visiting from warmer climates, not used to the winters in northern countries, will feel cold much sooner than locals will.

1.2   Psychological Factors of Microclimate Experience: 'Ambiance'

Beside the 'hard' physical factors, how we experience the microclimate is also affected by how we experience our surroundings. Influences such as the 'ambiance' of a place are part of this experience. American scientists did an experiment in the 1980s; demonstrating people's estimate of the temperature in a space differs depending on its ambiance. For this experiment people were placed in a climate chamber, heated to exactly 20

Influence of ambiance on micro-climate experience

°C. They were asked how they experienced the climate in this room. The first subjects visited the room in its original setting, with a sterile and technical look. Then the climate chamber had a cosy makeover, with carpeting and comfortable furniture. In this setting, subject estimated the air temperature to be much higher, while in fact it was exactly the same.

In a different experiment, people had a heater installed in their new desk, all set at the same temperature. The scientists told half of the subjects about this heater in their desk, and did not tell the other half. Most of the people who knew about the heater gave higher temperature estimations than those who did not know. Whether someone is outside alone or with other people also has an effect on the way the microclimate is experienced. Last but not least, the mood someone is in influences this person's experience of the microclimate.

These examples show that thermal comfort is not just the result of physical factors, but that much of it is 'in our heads'. So the 'ambiance' of a place, determined by such things as size, colours and materials, is also part of people's microclimate experience. Creating different 'ambiances' through design can make a difference in how the microclimate is perceived.

Influence of expectations and mood on temperature experience

6 A different type of hammam – the grotto behind a waterfall in Sonsbeek park in the Netherlands

2
Factors Determining the Urban Climate

To design for the urban climate, you need to know about a few basic processes, because virtually every urban design intervention in the spatial layout and use of materials changes the microclimate of an environment. Think of shadow patterns created by built elements and plants, the longwave radiation of building materials, and the way buildings change the way the wind flows. This makes each city, and each spot in it with its own spatial configuration, unique. The urban climate and microclimate also change constantly: per day, with each season and because of climate change. Therefore, designers and planners should keep the basic processes of the urban climate in mind and design for specific spots and their temporary climatic dynamics. These dynamics can mean that processes can be a problem in one situation, while they can be a potential in another. Wind, for instance, can sometimes be a nuisance, while it can bring much needed ventilation in other situations. The complexity of these processes can be an exciting and inspiring planning and design challenge for the 'makers' of the city.

As we know from the first chapter, two aspects are vital to the physical part of people's microclimate experience: the sensation of temperature, meaning everything that has to do with temperature; and the sensation of wind, meaning everything that has to do with air movement. For a considerable part, urban climatic processes determine the sensation of temperature and wind. This chapter is about these influences. Because all air movements are basically the result of differences in temperature, the processes relating to temperature are discussed before those relating to wind. The psychological influences on microclimate experience will be discussed at the end of this chapter.

The urban climate knows a number of factors that apply to different scale levels, but are inextricably connected. For example, small-scale microclimatic changes usually only have a very small local effect, like slight changes to the wind's course; but because there are so many buildings and other vertical structures in the city, these effects 'add up' and the city's wind field is ultimately changed. Another example is the addition of green elements. A few extra trees or green facades does not result in a lower air temperature for the city as a whole, but planting many trees in many places does have such an effect. A typical characteristic of the climate is its volatility, as we can see when we look at the wind. Wind is very chaotic and small changes in the city can bring sudden changes to its course, a typical example of the so-called butterfly effect. These changes come with certain uncertainties, but there are many reasonably predictable flow patterns. The most predictable processes of the urban climate belong to the thermal environment: light, shadow and air temperature. You can also make pretty good predictions about the psychological factors influencing microclimate experience that are determined by the 'ambiance' of a space. Because the urban climate factors differ so much in their predictability, I will mainly discuss average conditions and only a few extreme circumstances.

2.1   Urban Structure and Temperature Regimes

Shortwave solar radiation

The urban structure and its complexity of buildings, roads, green areas, water bodies and relief, as well as human activities such as traffic and industry have a great impact on the local thermal climate, which clearly differs from the climate in rural areas. This urban climate obviously has a significant influence on people's temperature experience. I will now explain which aspects play a role here.

2.1.1   Radiation and Heat

The basis of all thermal processes on earth is the incoming radiation from the sun (see illustration 7). This radiation can appear close to the earth's surface in several forms, after the

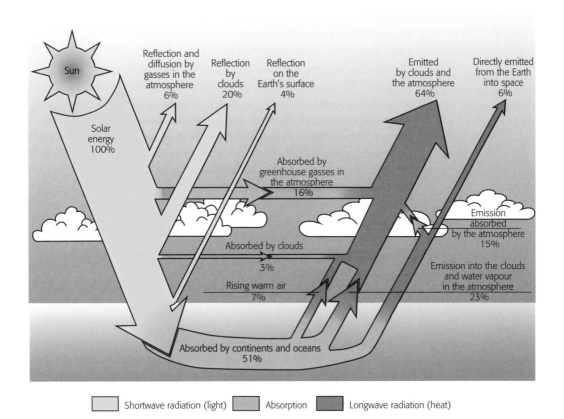

Reflection and diffusion by gasses in the atmosphere 6%

Reflection by clouds 20%

Reflection on the Earth's surface 4%

Emitted by clouds and the atmosphere 64%

Directly emitted from the Earth into space 6%

Solar energy 100%

Absorbed by greenhouse gasses in the atmosphere 16%

Emission absorbed by the atmosphere 15%

Absorbed by clouds 3%

Rising warm air 7%

Emission into the clouds and water vapour in the atmosphere 23%

Absorbed by continents and oceans 51%

Shortwave radiation (light) Absorption Longwave radiation (heat)

outer layer of the atmosphere and the clouds have reflected part of it. As shortwave radiation, it can hit objects on earth directly. Dust particles in the atmosphere can diffuse solar radiation and different types of surfaces can reflect it. When the earth or materials on it absorb the shortwave radiation, part of it is usually emitted later as longwave heat radiation and this is different for different materials. Many of these radiation processes are therefore influenced by the structure of the city.

Sun and shadow have the greatest effect on the temperature regimes of objects on earth. On a sunny, cloudless day in Central Europe, for example, a horizontal terrain will receive no less than 1000 watt per square metre at noon. On cloudy days, this is only 500 watt per square metre and in a building's shadow a mere 100 watt remain. So the effect of shadow on the incoming radiation is enormous. This effect obviously depends on the characteristics of the elements casting the shadow as well. Buildings and other non-transparent objects cast deep shadows. Transparent objects and trees will offer less shade, but, depending on the denseness of the foliage, they provide little to a lot of shade.

Besides the prominent aspect shadow, the altitude angle of solar rays influences the strength of the incoming radiation. This angle of direct solar rays varies, depending on the location on earth and the time of year. Close to the poles, the sun's angle

7 Types of radiation in the atmosphere and at the earth's surface

Sun and shadow

The sun's altitude angle

is always lower than at the equator. A lower angle means the incoming energy is spread out over a larger surface, thus creating less warmth per square metre. Illustration 8 shows the sun's altitude angle close to the equator, practically at right angles to the earth's surface. The radiation is divided over a surface at a 1:1 ratio. The sun's altitude angle is lower in temperate climate zones. As the illustration shows, the incoming radiation is spread out over a 1,4 times larger surface. Close to the poles, the radiation is even spread out over a surface twice as large, causing it to be much colder. The time of year is also an important factor in the altitude angle. This will be explained for a location near the 52nd latitude, the location of many European and American cities (see illustration 9). On the shortest day of the year in winter, the sun is at its lowest position, and therefore the altitude angle is at its smallest. The sun's path is also at its shortest. It rises more towards the southeast and sets in the southwest, whereas on the longest day, June 21st, the sun's position is much higher and its path is much longer. The sun then rises towards the northeast and sets in the northwest. In winter, shadow patterns are longer than in summer.

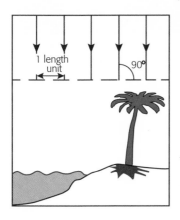 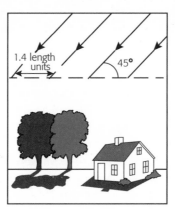 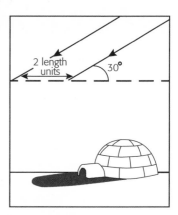

8 *Different angles of the sun in different parts of the world*

___

How materials reflect radiation

___

Part of the radiation falling on objects is reflected and part of it is absorbed. How much radiation surfaces reflect depends mostly on how light and smooth they are. The lighter and smoother the surface, the more reflection. Because, with objects with light and smooth surfaces, the radiation does not reach the mass underneath, the material will warm up more slowly. The reflectivity is usually expressed in a percentage of the total of the incoming radiation; the term for this percentage is *albedo*. In cities, many different materials are used; so knowing about their reflectivity can help regulate incoming solar radiation (see list, illustration 10).

How materials store and radiate heat

___

All materials have different heat storage and release charact-eristics. Emissivity plays a big role here. The term *emissivity* describes the ability of materials to release stored heat in the form of longwave radiation. Different materials release this

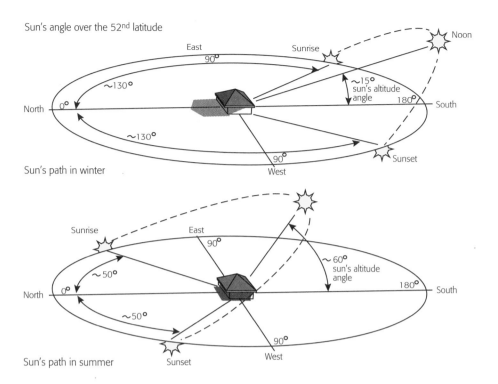

Sun's angle over the 52nd latitude

North — 0° — East — 90° — ~130° — Sunrise — ~15° sun's altitude angle — 180° — South — Noon
~130° — 90° — West — Sunset

Sun's path in winter

North — 0° — Sunrise — East — 90° — ~50° — ~60° sun's altitude angle — 180° — South
~50° — 90° — West — Sunset

Sun's path in summer

longwave thermal radiation in different quantities and at different speeds (see list, illustration 10). Most building materials, for example, have a high emissivity – they can store heat and release it well. Metals on the other hand possess this quality to a far lesser extent, because they conduct heat.

When an object has a larger surface than another object at the same location has, it of course receives more shortwave radiation, and it can also emit more longwave radiation. Cities have a large number of vertical surfaces – the walls of the buildings – and thus have more surface area to receive and emit radiation than an open landscape does. But even within a city there are great differences. A very densely built high-rise area has a much larger vertical surface area than a sprawling residential neighbourhood, with villas surrounded by large gardens. The high-rise area therefore stores much more radiation, emitting it later as heat.

Materials also have different levels of thermal conductivity. The term *thermal conductivity* reflects how fast a material can take up and release heat. This too we know from our daily experiences. A hot, metal pan, for example, releases the heat much faster than a stone brought to the same temperature. Materials conducting heat very slowly are also good for insulation. Air is a bad conductor of heat, that is why materials containing a lot of air, such as hollow concrete blocks or polystyrene foam, are such good insulators.

9 *The sun's path over the 52nd latitude*

Thermal conductivity of materials

Types of surfaces/ materials	Albedo of shortwave radiation	Emissivity	Thermal conductivity
Asphalt	5-20%	95%	higher
Grey concrete	10-35%	71-95%	higher
White concrete	71%	71-95%	higher
Red brick wall	20-40%	~90%	intermediate
Natural stone, bright	20-35%	~90%	higher
Wood, freshly planed	40%	90%	very low
Tar paper	8-18%	92%	
Roof tiles	10-35%	90%	intermediate
Slate	10%	90%	higher
Corrugated iron	10-16%	13-28%	high
Iron/ Steel, polished	~80%	~15%	very high
Glass	10-50%	~90%	higher
White wall paint/ plaster	70-95%	~90%	
Black wall paint	2-15%	~95%	
Sandy soil	25-45%	76%	low
Gravel paving	72%	28%	low
Open soil, dark	7-10%	90-98%	low
Grass/ lawn	15-25%	90-95%	low
Water (high sun angle)	3-10%	98%	intermediate
Water (low sun angle)	~80%	98%	intermediate

10 *List of albedo, emissivity and thermal conductivity of different materials*

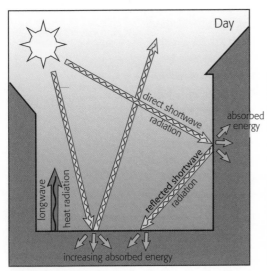
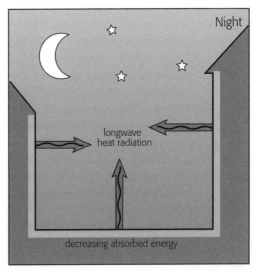

11 *Radiation flows in an urban street canyon*

The factors albedo, emissivity and thermal conductivity have a great influence on thermoregulation in cities. Therefore, the choices of building materials (brick, timber, concrete, steel, plastic, et cetera) or the materials in landscape design (stone, earth, water, vegetation) are an important part of urban climate design (illustration 10).

The configuration of buildings is another influence on the level of longwave thermal radiation. In densely built-up areas, this radiation can't get away, because it is bounced back and forth between the buildings. As a result, these areas cool off much more slowly than open areas do. The closer the buildings stand together, the more the upward horizon is restricted; a phenomenon termed the *sky view factor*. Areas with a low sky view factor, like a street with tall buildings, hold on to more of the thermal radiation. Eventually, this results in higher air temperatures.

Retaining thermal radiation in the city

2.1.2 Air Temperature

Air temperature is the best-known phenomenon of the climate. For the sake of convenience, air temperature is called 'temperature' in weather forecasts, even though this term is not very accurate. As we saw from earlier sections, we are surrounded by many more phenomena influencing the way we experience temperature, such as radiation. The large-scale high- and low-pressure areas they show in the weather forecasts mainly determine the air temperature. In cities, however, thermal radiation clearly also has a role in warming the air. Besides these factors, water evaporation and anthropogenic (human-made) heat influence the air temperature in the city.

The amount of water evaporating into the air has an effect on the air temperature. Solar and thermal radiation cause water to evaporate. The evaporation process extracts energy from the air, as a result of which its temperature can't rise as fast. People often speak of the cooling effect of water vapour, but strictly speaking we should speak of a reduced warming of the air due to evaporation. Water bodies and soils containing water have a high level of evaporation at their surface and make the air warm up more slowly. Paving the soil and channelling waterways, thus reducing their surface area, will lead to substantially less evaporation in the city, making the air warm up faster.

Water evaporation tempers the air temperature

At the surface of their leaves, plants evaporate a lot of water. This happens through the supply of water from the roots to the stomata of the leaves. As a result, areas with more vegetation heat up less quickly than the stony areas in the city.

Another heat factor in the city is the so-called anthropogenic heat. This involves the heat production directly resulting from human activity. Think of heat produced by heaters in buildings, escaping because of the buildings' bad insulation. But also

Urban functions raise the air temperature

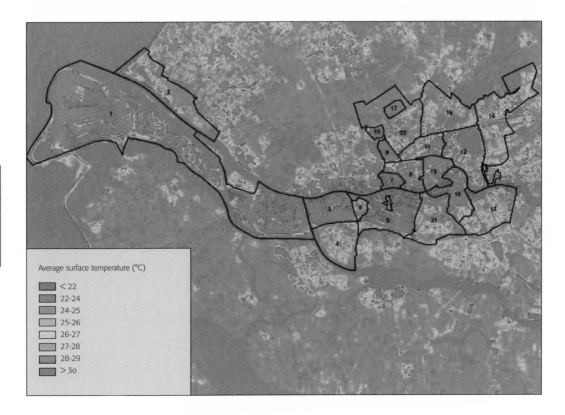

12 *Infrared image of surface temperatures in the Dutch city of Rotterdam, clearly showing the heat archipelago*

think of air conditioners cooling houses or cars, since they give off much heat to the outside air. The production processes in commercial and industrial zones also generate extra heat. The same goes for power plants, as they often produce residual heat. Cars' motors also produce extra heat, and busy, narrow roads can heat up considerably because of this.

2.1.3 Temperature Phenomena Typical for the Urban Environment

Urban heat islands

In the previous sections many aspects were discussed that demonstrate that there is a different climate in the city than in most natural landscapes, and that a densely built-up city is usually warmer than its surroundings. This is the result of retained longwave thermal radiation, anthropogenic heat and reduced evaporation (because of a lack of open soil surfaces, water and plants). This heat phenomenon is therefore called the *urban heat island* effect. This term is very concise, and it does not reflect the differences in temperature within the city, depending on the building density, paving, green and water. A green, loosely built-up residential area with large gardens or a city park with tall trees can even be cooler than the adjacent landscape. And a densely built-up and completely paved industrial zone at the edge of the city can often be warmer than a less built-up city centre. It is therefore more suitable to use the term *heat archipelago* to indicate that cities can contain various heat areas and that it does

36

not always concern the whole city or the central areas
(see illustration 12).

Urban heat islands occur both in summer and in winter.
During the winter, this is mainly the result of anthropogenic
heat, going on day and night. In temperate climate zones, there
is much less solar radiation (the greatest source of thermal
radiation) in the winter, so radiation does not heat up the air
so much. During the summer, however, especially radiation is
responsible for the urban heat island effect. The radiation is
mostly received and stored during the day, and it is released as
longwave radiation at night. In the daytime, urban heat islands
are a little warmer than the countryside. At night, however, there
is a big difference in air temperature. As discussed before, this
is due to the permanent release of longwave radiation by all
those buildings, thus preventing the air from cooling off. The
summer heat island effect is strongest on hot, cloudless days with
little wind. Measurements have shown that the difference in air
temperature between heat islands and cooler areas of the city or
the surrounding land can be as large as 12 °C on nights like these.
Especially during heat waves, with several hot days in a row,
problems can arise because the heat can build up over the days.

*Urban heat
phenomena
through time*

People often say warmer cities are nice, because you do
not need as much heating in winter, and people have fewer
problems with ice and snow, plus that these cities improve
outdoor urban life. In the end, though, the problems connected
to urban heat are bigger. Heat stress leads to inevitable health
issues (see chapter 1); food spoils faster when it's warm; insect
pests such as ticks and mosquitoes thrive in hot summers; and
blue-green algae in urban water bodies can pose health risks as
well. Heat also causes problems with infrastructure: asphalt wears
out and deforms; and moving parts of bridges and such can
malfunction because of expansion.

*Problems due
to urban heat
phenomena*

2.2 Wind in the Urban Environment

It is important to get to know urban wind patterns, because
urban design can have a great impact on these patterns. But first,
we need to discuss a few basic principles of how wind evolves.
Wind is caused by differences in temperature. Warm air is lighter
than cold air, because there is more space between the air's
molecules. The warm air rises, while the heavier cool air tends
to stay closer to the earth's surface. This rising of warm air
causes underpressure, sucking in cooler air. This is how air
movement, or wind, comes about. On a large scale, we can see
this phenomenon as wind occurring between high- and low-
pressure areas, being warmer and cooler bodies of air. On this
large scale, the Earth's rotation plays a role in the direction of

*How differences
in temperature
generate wind*

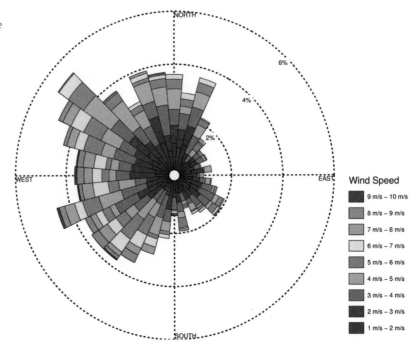

13 *Wind rose for Detroit City Airport, USA during the fall 2010 period*

Wind Speed

■ 9 m/s – 10 m/s
■ 8 m/s – 9 m/s
□ 7 m/s – 8 m/s
□ 6 m/s – 7 m/s
■ 5 m/s – 6 m/s
■ 4 m/s – 5 m/s
■ 3 m/s – 4 m/s
■ 2 m/s – 3 m/s
■ 1 m/s – 2 m/s

the prevailing winds. The focus of this book is on the temperate climate zones. In these zones, the prevailing winds on the northern hemisphere are usually south-western, and on the southern hemisphere they are usually north-western.

On smaller, local scales, weaker wind systems develop between warmer and cooler areas. We can observe these wind systems on days when the large-scale wind is very weak. Most days, however, the influences of the large-scale wind systems prevail, as these are usually much stronger than the small, local wind systems. The wind and its strength and direction in weather forecasts regard the large-scale systems. To understand wind in urban climates, you do not need to know everything about the complex large-scale wind systems. Just take an area's general wind data into consideration (you can usually find these on the websites of national weather institutes or the local airports, see illustration 13).

Wind flows in the city are not the same as those in open landscapes

All wind flows have to change direction when they hit obstacles, including cities. Because of this, wind slows down on the leeside of objects, whereas it speeds up in narrow places, where it is compressed. These winds can be gusty and change direction abruptly. Stronger winds and bigger obstacles like tall buildings increase the intensity of these gusts. Local topographical differences can also induce small-scale wind in and around cities. This can happen for instance when a city is located next to a large body of water or in a hilly area. Closely built-up areas in a city, generating heat, can also induce local airflows.

2.2.1 Local Wind Systems

As described above in broad outlines, wind arises because of differences in air temperature, whereby warm air rises and cooler air is sucked in. In cities, three phenomena can cause these differences in temperature: the difference in air temperature over land and over water; in hills and in valleys, warming up at different speeds; and the differences in air temperature in urban heat islands and in cooler areas. In line with these temperature differences, coastal cities deal with coastal wind systems; cities with relief have hill-valley winds; and all cities have breezes between warmer and cooler parts of the city.

In summer, when the large-scale wind systems are weak, local wind systems arise in coastal cities. These are generated by the different speeds at which water and landmasses warm up. During the day, water takes more time to warm up than land does. So the air over land is warmer and it starts to rise around midday. This in turn causes underpressure, sucking in the cooler sea air. This means the wind blows from the sea towards the land. So, during the day, cooler air comes into the city. At night, it is the other way around, because water cools off more slowly than land does. Then, the water is warmer than the land is, and the wind blows from the land towards the sea (see illustration 14). The direction of the coastal wind systems is more or less perpendicular to the coastline. When it is exceptionally hot and there are no obstacles, such as mountain ranges, these sea breezes can reach almost a hundred kilometres inland. Typically,

The location and structure of the city induce small-scale wind systems

Coastal wind systems

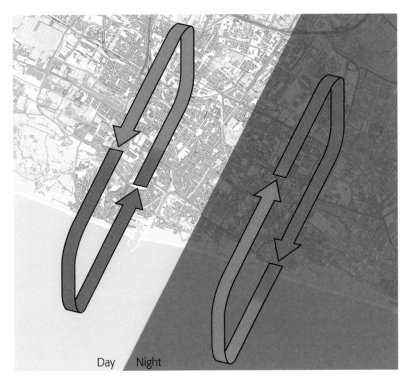

Day   Night

14 *Land and sea breezes during the day and at night*

though, these coastal wind systems are not very strong at all. In cities on the shores of large lakes, there can also be temperature differences between the water and the land, so there can be afternoon sea breezes in those cities too. On tranquil summer days, there is usually a bit more wind along the shores than at the middle of the lake. These breezes between land and water are generally relatively weak wind phenomena, which in any case can only develop on days without large-scale wind flows.

Valley wind systems

When a city has hills and valleys with differences in height of over 80 metres and gradients of at least 3 per cent, winds can develop. The time of day and different speeds at which surfaces in the hills and valleys warm up are important for the development of these winds. The slopes warm up more quickly than the valleys do, creating upward airflows (illustration 15, A). During the day, especially in the afternoons, there is an uphill breeze (B). At night, this phenomenon is reversed. The hilltops are more open than the valleys are, so they can radiate heat more easily (C). The air here cools off quickly. This cool air is heavier and moves to the lowest parts of the valleys. So now the airflow is downhill (D).

The opener the hilltops (for example grassland), the faster they can produce cold air through accelerated radiation. More cold air will flow downhill. This air then flows close to the ground and moves slowly, normally no more than 2 metres per second. Obstacles, such as buildings, mounds and dense planting, can halt these slow airflows because they do not have enough speed to pass by or over the obstacles. The obstacles block the potentially cooling valley breezes, which could have otherwise gone on to the warmer parts of the city. Therefore, it is advisable to keep these areas free from obstacles.

Urban heat islands can also create airflows themselves. The air over the warmer parts of the city rises, and air from a nearby

15 *Valley wind systems during the day and at night*

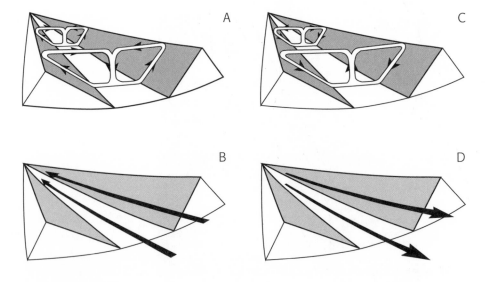

A

C

B

D

40

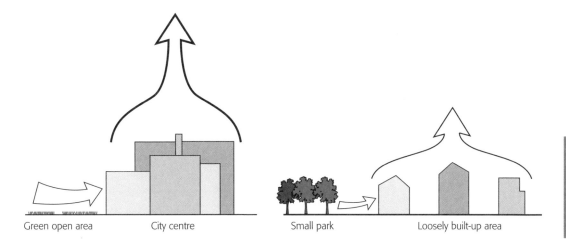

Green open area   City centre   Small park   Loosely built-up area

cooler area is sucked in. The bigger the difference in temperature, the more cool air is sucked in, resulting in more wind. The airflow between a densely built-up city centre and a large, 'cool' open park, for instance, can be stronger, whereas a breeze between a small park and a loosely built-up residential area will only ever be light (see illustration 16). If cool breezes are given the space to flow, they can find their way into the warm areas of a city, thus providing ventilation. But these airflows are weak too and unable to pass higher obstacles.

All these local airflows can provide natural ventilation for the city. Their effect manifests itself especially on hot summer days and nights, so precisely when it is most wanted. To give these breezes the space they need, we should make sure the areas where the cool air originates from and the ventilation axes are kept open (more on this subject in section 4.2). On days with more unstable weather and stronger large-scale wind, this wind will force these small-scale airflows apart, so they will not be able to manifest themselves. The city does not need extra ventilation on those days anyways, because there is enough wind as it is.

2.2.2 Speed of the Large-Scale Wind Around Cities

Close to the ground, obstacles or the so-called 'roughness' of the earth's surface slow down the large-scale wind. Water surfaces are quite smooth, but on land, plants and relief make the surface more rugged. Similar to other spatial volumes on the earth's surface, like mountains and woods, cities with their buildings and tall vegetation usually form an obstacle that the wind has to flow around. A city with many tall buildings standing quite close together will be a bigger obstacle than a city with many low-rise buildings. Despite these differences, the average wind speed in urban areas is around 30-50 per cent lower than outside of the city. At densely built-up cities with high-rise buildings, large-scale

16 *Urban wind between warm and cool areas with different temperature gradients*

Urban wind systems

Wind speeds are different in cities and open landscapes

wind is deflected up to a height of 500 metres over the roofs (see illustration 17). Occasionally, this can be even higher, seeing that the tallest skyscrapers are over 800 metres high. Only above it does the wind regain its original speed.

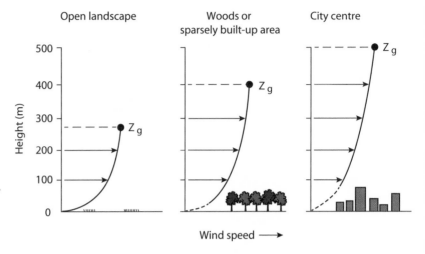

17 Profile of large-scale wind over open land-scapes, woods or sparsely built-up areas and densely built-up cities

Wind flow patterns are different in cities and open landscapes

From the above, one could unjustly conclude that wind is not an issue in cities, because of the lower wind speeds. Nothing could be further from the truth. Due to the combination of topography, buildings of various heights and openings in the urban structure, wind is deflected and compressed in many ways, making it very strong in certain places. Wind flows can also break off or speed up abruptly. In the city, wind is in fact much more turbulent and changeable than in an open landscape or over sea. What the flow patterns look like in the city and how strong the wind will be at certain spots, is different for each location. To get an idea of the airflow patterns on a small scale, you need to carefully study the spatial volumes of each individual location.

2.2.3 Typical Wind Patterns in the Urban Environment

Wind flow patterns are different for each location, but they do have a lot in common

Although the flow patterns of wind in cities always depend on local contexts with their unique building configurations, there are a number of flow principles that normally occur around certain building volumes and in certain open spaces. These patterns occur at several spots around volumes and come with either reduced or increased wind flows. The height, width and length of the volumes determine what the patterns look like. It's interesting to know that, in principle, wind shows the same flow patterns on small and large scales. That is why many patterns have no scale and are not expressed in absolute, but in relative numbers. Knowing about the patterns discussed in this section can help you predict wind patterns on a local level for many locations.

Wind experts know wind patterns can be hard to predict and quantitative data on speeds can be hard to calculate.

This goes especially for combined volumes of buildings, relief or vegetation. Special simulation or wind tunnel experiments are needed here (see chapter 5 as well). But with a 'sense' for assessing flow patterns (through observing water flows, plumes of smoke and dust, see illustration 18 as well), and knowing about flow patterns around freestanding buildings, you can make simple predictions about wind patterns around clusters of buildings. You could, for example, take the estimated patterns for freestanding buildings in maps or profiles, and overlap these, as it were. This can provide you with a lot of information about the interactions that are to be expected.

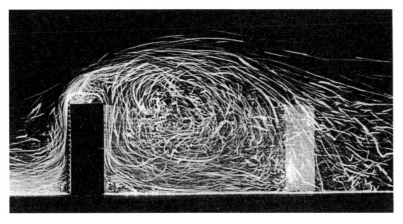

18 *In a wind tunnel, fine dust is blown around a building volume to see how the wind flows*

First of all, I will sketch a number of patterns that occur around single volumes like vegetation and buildings, then those around simple building clusters, and finally the wind patterns typical for open urban spaces, such as streets and squares. The wind in these sketches always has the same direction. In reality, this is obviously not the case, but this is not a problem when predicting these patterns. When you need to look into the flow patterns for a different direction, you simply project the patterns for this other direction. It is, however, very important to keep in mind that we are talking about some basic patterns here, and there are many possible variations. Of course, the relief of a city is also of great influence on the wind patterns in it, particularly if there are big differences in height. For example, a mountain range on the leeside of a city can deflect large-scale wind and thus decrease the wind speeds in the city itself. In a coastal city, on the other hand, the wind can be much stronger. But also in these situations, the general small-scale flow patterns are still the same, if it is only the wind speed that is lower.

Vegetation clusters as you can find in a city park come in several typical shapes, such as line-shaped in lanes or wider in tree clumps or groves. Depending on the 'depth' of such a volume of vegetation, typical wind patterns form. The following phenomena occur at line-shaped shelterbelts:

1   At the windward side, there is a small sheltered area close to the ground (illustration 19, 1).
2   On the sides, wind speeds are clearly increased, forming the so-called *corner streams* (more on this subject under 'freestanding buildings'). This is because of the compression of air flowing around the shelterbelt (illustration 19, 2).
3   On the leeside behind the shelterbelt, the pressure is lower and there is a large sheltered area (illustration 19, 3), in which it takes the wind up to a maximum of thirty times the height of the trees to reach its original speed. In general, the length of the sheltered area at substantially lower wind speeds (less than half) is about five times the height of the trees.

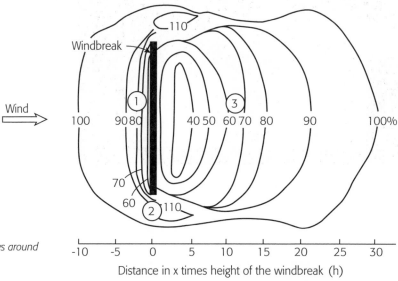

19 *Wind flows around a shelterbelt*

Distance in x times height of the windbreak (h)

Broader groves have much smaller sheltered areas behind them (see illustration 20). When the trees in a grove have similar tops forming sort of a 'flat roof', the sheltered area behind the grove is smaller. When the grove has a more irregular 'roof', the sheltered area is somewhat larger. When the canopy of foliage is not very dense and the trees have high tops, the wind can flow through the top and trunk part of the grove, but the sheltered area behind it will be much longer.

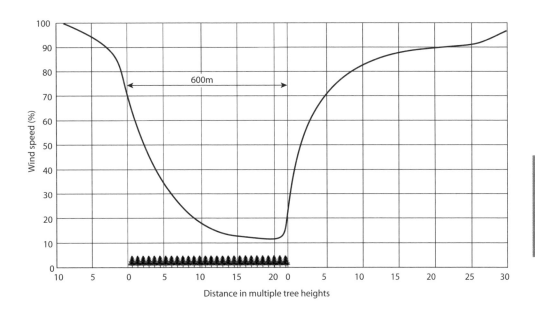

Wind speed (%)

Distance in multiple tree heights

Around freestanding buildings of medium height at right angles to the wind, the following flow patterns arise:

1 On the windward side a little above the middle of the building front, you get eddies due to the bouncing of the wind (illustration 21a, 1).
2 A way off the foot of the building, at the windward side, there is a small sheltered area, where the main flows are divided (illustration 21b, 2).
3 At the sides of the building, there are corner streams with higher wind speeds, due to the compression of the air flowing around the building (illustration 21b, 3).
4 On the leeward side behind the building, the pressure is lower and there is a sheltered area (illustration 21b, 4), the size of which depends on the height of the building. In general, the sheltered area with lower wind speeds is about three to five times the height of the building. But the 'depth' of the building also plays a part – as the depth increases, the sheltered area behind the building becomes smaller. Some air does flow back here, which can cause turbulence. Further away from the building, the wind speed increases again.

Around freestanding, tall building volumes of over 20 metres, at right angles to the direction of the wind, other prominent phenomena occur as well:

1 Extra corner streams develop at the top (illustration 22a, 1).
2 At the windward side of the building, winds blowing over the rooftops at higher speeds are 'scooped' down, as it were (illustration 22a, 2). This phenomenon is called *downwash*, and at the pedestrian level, it can be the cause of substantially higher and sometimes even dangerous wind speeds.

20 *Wind profiles for different types of groves*

Wind patterns around freestanding buildings of medium height at right angles to the wind

Wind patterns around tall buildings at right angles to the wind

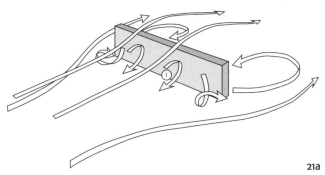
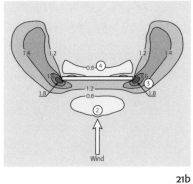

21a   21b

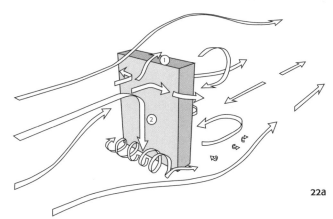
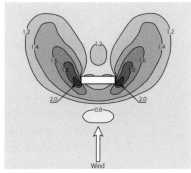

22a   22b

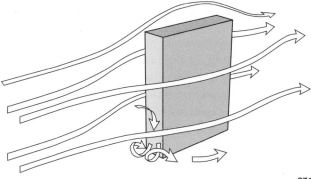
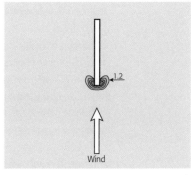

23a   23b

21 Wind flows around a freestanding medium height building, with percentages of increase and decrease in speed in relation to the original wind speed

22 Wind flows around a freestanding high-rise building, with percentages of increase and decrease in speed in relation to the original wind speed

23 Wind flows around a building parallel to the wind direction, with percentages of increase and decrease in speed in relation to the original wind speed

46

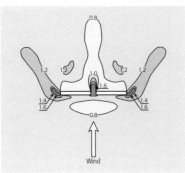

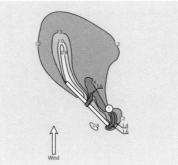

24

25

When buildings are parallel to the direction of the wind, the flows are deflected considerably less. The air pressure at the windward side is much smaller and there are hardly any corner streams. The sheltered area behind the building is much shorter too.

Wind patterns around buildings parallel to the wind direction

When wind hits buildings with passageways, other patterns occur. The wind hitting the building is also forced through the small opening of the passage. This creates a compression of airflows and thus high wind speeds, which can sometimes be quite dangerous for pedestrians and cyclists.

Wind patterns around passageways

When buildings are diagonal to the prevailing wind, even stronger corner stream areas develop at the windward side than around buildings that are at right angles to the wind. These corner stream areas then start to interact (illustration 25, 1). Eddies around these buildings can also be stronger.

Wind patterns around buildings at an angle with the wind direction

The examples depicted here mainly represent slab-shaped buildings. For 'deeper' buildings, the flows are somewhat different. The chief effect of 'deeper' buildings is a smaller sheltered area. The deeper the building, the smaller the sheltered area. Illustration 26 shows how the sheltered areas change with the depth of buildings. The buildings are divided into basic cubes without a scale, indicated as a size 'L'. The diagram shows how many times 'L' the sheltered area behind the buildings will approximately be as the buildings become deeper. The illustration only reflects the changes in the total sheltered area, not the wind speed reduction percentages.

When buildings are grouped together different flow patterns develop, because of the interaction between the flows around the individual buildings. These patterns are usually relatively hard to predict, but you can estimate what some simple patterns will approximately look like, based on the estimated size of the

Estimating the interaction between wind patterns around groups of buildings

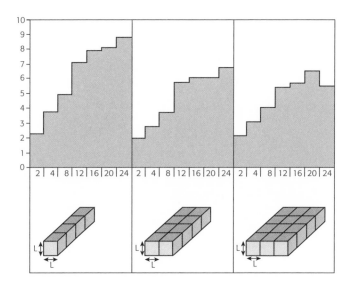

26 *Diagram with different building depths and the expected sheltered areas at their leeside*

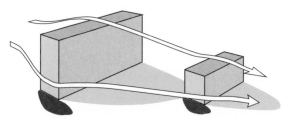

27 *Buildings at a distance from each other with slightly interacting wind flows*

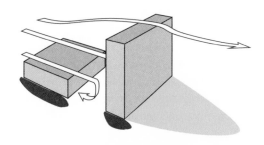

28 *Buildings with clearly interacting wind flows*

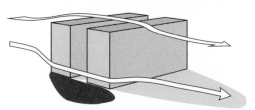

29 *Buildings with clearly interacting flows and corner streams*

corner streams. When the corner streams around freestanding buildings overlap as it were, you can expect higher wind speeds. This also influences the wind directions around the buildings. The examples in illustrations 28 and 29 show that flow patterns around buildings lined up at short distances from each other have more interaction than those around buildings with more space between them or buildings that are alternately configured (illustration 27).

48

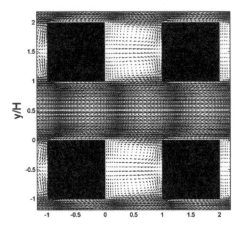

30 *Wind flows in a street*

The wind climate in open spaces like the streets and squares in a city is mostly influenced by the volumes of the surrounding buildings. The airflows around the individual buildings interact here as well, generating higher wind speeds and other spatial patterns. Continuous building configuration along the streets can have a channelling effect on the wind, if the street is more or less parallel to the prevailing wind direction. This effect especially occurs in streets with long, straight axes and smooth facades. We can also see this channelling effect when the buildings are more spaced out, but the effect is not as strong (see illustration 30). If broad streets or squares gradually become narrower, the wind is compacted and its speed increases even more.

Channelling effect of wind flows in streets and on longish squares

The proportions of open spaces such as streets and squares have a significant impact on the wind patterns. Especially the ratio between the height (H) of the buildings and the width (W) of the areas between the buildings is of influence. With the wind direction at right angles to the buildings, typical flow patterns develop for different types of proportions (see illustration 31). You will find *skimming flows* in relatively narrow streets. This means most of the wind flow stays above the rooftops, leaving a

Proportions of streets and squares and typical wind flow regimes

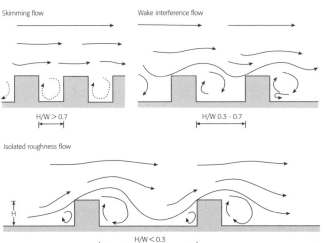

Skimming flow   Wake interference flow

H/W > 0.7   H/W 0.3 - 0.7

Isolated roughness flow

H/W < 0.3

31 *Profiles of the three wind regimes: skimming flow, wake interference and isolated roughness flow*

49

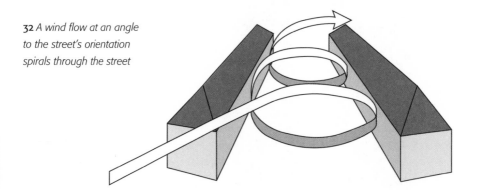

32 *A wind flow at an angle to the street's orientation spirals through the street*

relatively sheltered area between the buildings. When the street or square is wider (with H/W-ratios between 0.3 and 0.7), we see *wake interference flow* patterns: the sheltered areas behind the buildings overlap the small sheltered areas in front. We often find parallel eddies here, but the wind speeds are usually average. With H/W-ratios of 0.3 and smaller, the buildings are so far apart that wind can almost resume its original flow pattern and speed. This pattern is called *isolated roughness flow*. This type of flow regime often leads to wind nuisance on large squares.

Street length and direction with typical wind flows

The length of the street is also important for the wind climate in it. This works in a similar fashion as described above. Short streets with an H/W-ratio smaller than 0.3 do not have much wind flowing through them (when they are at right angles to the wind direction). Longer streets allow for the wind to quickly retain its original speed; we then see the channelling-effect we discussed before. This effect is significantly smaller when there are many trees in the street or when the facades alternate, one at least half a building depth in front of the other. When the wind comes in at an angle, spiralling whirls often occur, swirling through the streets (see illustration 32).

Wind flows on squares

Squares are obviously not just 'enlarged streets'; they usually have a number of openings, for instance at the entrances of the surrounding streets. The larger these entrances, the easier the large-scale wind regains its original speed on pedestrian level. Also, the buildings at squares are often of different heights. On old European church squares, for example, the downwash-effect of church towers is a common phenomenon. The varied geometry of urban squares results in more complex flow patterns than those in streets, and it is impossible to generalize. Like before, however, it *is* possible to use estimations of corner streams and sheltered areas to gain some insight into the estimated flow patterns. Likewise, the H/W-ratios and their different wind regimes (skimming flow, wake interference and isolated roughness flow) can help you predict the wind patterns on different kinds of squares.

2.3　Ambiance and Microclimate Experience

Besides all physical factors, urban space also has an indirect effect on how people experience the microclimate. The ambiance of an environment plays an important part here. A space can have a 'warm' or 'cold' ambiance even if its physical characteristics do not produce this effect. This is the effect of environmental psychology on people's experience. For example: through associations in people's minds, visual impressions can influence what they estimate the microclimate to be like, without being directly exposed to it. These 'ambiance aspects' encompass the openness of spaces, colours and materials. Some of these aspects have a clear relation to physical effects on the microclimate, and some have no physical effect whatsoever. You can use these 'ambiance characteristics' to manipulate people's thermal experience somewhat.

My own research showed that people from different cultural backgrounds have different associations with these atmospheric aspects. People from the Middle East, for instance, regarded certain materials and colours as 'comfortable', which can indeed provide for a better thermal comfort in the hot climates of that area (like smooth tiles in a light colour), but which can often be counterproductive in cooler climates.

Many people associate a spacious and open urban area with a low H/W-ratio (below 0,25) with wind and exposure to the elements. This perception often coincides with microclimatic circumstances typical for such spaces. In cooler climates the

The ambiance of cities' outdoor spaces influences the microclimate experience

People from different cultures experience ambiance and the microclimate differently

33 *A square that is too spacious: Binnenrotte in Rotterdam, the Netherlands*

34 *'Cold materials' in Lille*

Perception of spatial proportions of outdoor areas

Perception of the materials in urban spaces

Perception of colours in urban outdoor spaces

wind is predominant in these spacious and open areas, and in warmer climates excessive solar radiation is. The fact that people consciously regard these types of spaces as unpleasant (thus often avoiding them), plus the fact that the microclimate indeed often is problematic, requires adaptation measures.

The materials used in urban spaces have a big influence on the thermal experience. People especially associate the way materials feel when you touch them with 'warm' and 'cold'. People perceive materials with a low thermal conductivity, such as wood and bricks, as 'warm', and steel, glass and concrete as 'cold'. Materials with a smooth surface, such as enamel and tiles, are usually considered 'cold' as well, particularly in countries with a temperate or cool climate. This could be because these 'cold' materials, as opposed to materials with a softer surface, have no insulating layers of air, making the material feel warmer upon touch. It could also be because of the thermal conductivity of the materials. But what's clear is that people do not need to touch the materials to make this association. People often only need to see the materials (for example on higher parts of buildings' facades) to make these associations. So for the connection to thermal experience, it does not really matter if people are in direct contact with the used materials or not.

As we all know, colours have a great influence on the 'ambiance' as well. Colours call up certain associations in different cultures, and are often described as 'warm' or 'cold/cool'. In the Western world, people often perceive colours with many yellow or red tones as 'warm' colours. These associations

52

are the result of a symbolic connection to warm elements such as fire and the sun, which have yellow and red tones as well. Blue, white and grey, on the other hand, are usually associated with 'cool'. This is probably because of a symbolic connection to water, ice and clouds, representing cold weather situations. In other cultures, these associations are different.

Nonetheless, these colours in fact have nothing to do with the physical thermal characteristics of materials. However, how light a colour is *does* influence the albedo, and thus the reflection of light and the absorption of heat. So, whether something has a 'warm' or a 'cold' colour does not make any difference to the microclimate – but it *does* make a difference for the ambiance and whether people perceive a space as warm or cold.

35 *The 'Ice palace' as people call it, in The Hague, the Netherlands*

3

Mapping the Urban Climate at a City Scale

Planning and design can influence the urban climate on the scale of the entire city. Before we start making concrete plans or designs for a whole city or larger parts of it, however, we need to get an overview of the current situation. Every city and every neighbourhood has a different climate, so we can't use generic solutions for all cities. The urban climate depends on the size of the city; its location, for example near the coast or in the mountains; the building morphology; and how 'green' the individual districts are. The characteristics of the urban climate for a specific city can be studied through several analysis techniques. These types of analyses as described in this chapter usually do not reflect the situation in small locations, but offer general indications about potentials and problems for the whole city with a differentiation down to the district level. These analyses are often summarized into an 'urban climate map', which forms a crucial basis for decisions about design, planning and policy.

There are various ways to analyse the urban climate. These depend on what exactly can be an urban climate problem or potential in a certain city; on the available data; and on the budget for the analyses. An urban climate analysis at the city-scale normally covers the whole urban area. The surroundings also have to be taken into account, because the urban climate obviously does not end at the city limits. The optimal method for an urban climate analysis would be to conduct measurements over a long period of time on very many locations, for instance in a grid of 100 x 100 metres and on different heights. Logistically and financially, though, this is not feasible. That is why spot check measurements are mostly used, in combination with other analysis techniques to thoroughly analyse the urban climate. Think of temperature maps, wind maps and 'urban climate maps' summarizing these analyses in a comprehensive system.

I will first describe these other techniques before we come to the additional measurement methods. Several countries have begun to analyse their cities' climates, some countries having started much sooner than others. Some cities already base their policies on these analyses. Examples from across the world will be discussed to show a broad range of urban climate analyses. For each analysis method, the specific goals are described, which aspects of the urban climate it reflects, what needs to be done in order to make the analysis, and whether specialist knowledge is required or not. This chapter ends with a discussion of vulnerability analyses that represent which people are vulnerable to the negative effects of the urban climate and at what times. These assessments are important too, since they can indicate at which places the urban climate has to be adapted urgently and at which places this can wait.

This chapter is also set up according to the themes of 'thermal environment' and 'wind'. The environmental psychology factors are left out, since they are less of a factor on this scale.

3.1 Climatope Maps as Indicators of Temperature

For relatively small cities in a fairly simple environment when it comes to relief, non-experts can make temperature maps, based on the classification of climatopes, a concept that will be described below. Experts do have to make analysis maps for very complicated urban areas, for instance when a city is located between mountains and the ocean. For many cities, however, the situation is not that complicated, and 'climatope maps' will suffice for an overview of the temperature situations.

The 'climatope' concept means that different types of areas and districts in a city have typical microclimatic characteristics. This entails for example the influence of the building structure,

What is a 'climatope'

vegetation, soil surfaces and anthropogenic heat in different areas of the city. The climatopes are mainly classified and named according to the land use, but partly also according to the building density. The maps with climatope divisions primarily tell you about the thermal behaviour of the different districts.

To be able to categorize the city into climatopes, you need to integrate information about land use, building structure, vegetation and surfacing. Land use is an important factor for the thermal characteristics of a district. Human activities can have an anthropogenic heat-impact on their environment, for instance through traffic, industrial residual heat, poorly insulated buildings and air conditioners; accounting for about 10 per cent of urban thermal conditions. Such sources of heat can be found in areas with much infrastructure; with factories; or for example with buildings with many air conditioners such as shopping malls, hospitals and hotels.

Determining factors for a climatope

The urban building structure is most important for the climatope classification. A high density and closed building structure, as you would find in city centres, results in a strong heat-absorption and limited ventilation. On the other side, areas where buildings are spread out, like garden cities, upscale residential areas and the city's periphery have a lower heat potential.

The density and type of vegetation is of great influence on the climatope classification as well. Planting usually has a tempering effect on the temperature. The more vegetation in a district, the larger the tempering effect can be. Because of their height and thus the deeper shadows they cast, trees and shrubs are more important for the tempering of temperature fluctuations than for instance allotment gardens, flowerbeds or lawns.

A final important factor is the use of materials. Materials in outdoor areas or on facades have a great effect on a city's thermoregulation, because of their different radiation characteristics and albedo. Surfacing can lead to accumulation of heat, especially if the heat gets trapped, like in narrow streets. You can use all these data to categorize the climatopes, connecting the various urban climate parameters. Below, you will find the main characteristics of the different climatopes.

Water climatopes with a width of at least 50 metres have a tempering effect on the air temperature. The slow warming and cooling of water levels temperature peaks, both high and low. In summer, this means the temperature during the day is lower than it is in the surrounding areas, and during the night it is higher. Because of this, land and sea breezes can develop near large water bodies, such as lakes. The atmospheric humidity near water bodies is higher, and there is more wind around large water bodies, because water surfaces do not intercept wind.

Water climatope

36 *Water climatope*

37 *'Open landscape' climatope*

38 *Forest climatope*

39 *Park climatope*

'Open landscape'
climatope

An 'open landscape' climatope, such as large, open fields, has relatively big temperature fluctuations over the course of a day. Because of the openness (sky view factor) of these landscapes, retained heat can radiate freely at night, quickly cooling the air. Therefore, these areas are often important 'producers' of cold airflows (see section 2.2.1). The wind is free to roam here, since there are few obstacles.

Forest climatope

Forests, but also large groves in parks, have tempered temperature fluctuations and fairly constant relative air humidity. This is caused by the shading and by the evaporation of water during the day, the retention of heat in the trunks and the reduced radiation during the night, keeping the woods warmer than the open landscape.

Park climatope

City parks and public gardens have more extreme temperature fluctuations per day than the built environment has. The bigger sky view factor in open areas allows the retained warmth to radiate at night and the air cools down. In parks with separate trees, it is a little cooler, because of the shadows and the evapotranspiration. These park-like areas are therefore often important 'producers' of lower air temperatures, which can cool the surroundings as well. Open green areas can also enhance ventilation.

40 *Garden city or village climatope*

41 *City periphery climatope*

42 *City climatope*

The garden city climatope has a low building-density of up to three building layers with large gardens with trees in them. The classical 'garden cities', but also villages and upscale residential are often typical for this category. The temperature fluctuation in these neighbourhoods is fairly tempered, clearly cooling down at night. The large share of open space enhances ventilation, which helps with the cooling.

Garden city climatope

City periphery climatopes are more built-up than the garden cities. This can range from freestanding houses of up to five floors or clustered development of up to three floors, such as terraced houses or perimeter block developments with a large courtyard. The nightly cooling is limited and the ventilation is often somewhat slowed by the buildings and the planting.

City periphery climatope

The city climatope is characterized by closed building configurations of high-rise and freestanding buildings. Often, this climatope can be found in historical city centres, but also many newer parts of cities. There is only limited vegetation, and thus also limited cooling through evaporation. In daytime, the area really heats up and at night, it only cools down a little bit. As a result, there is a clear heat island effect, most prominently felt at night.

City climatope

43 *City centre climatope*

44 *Commercial district climatope*

45 *Industrial estate climatope*

46 *Railway yard climatope*

City centre climatope

City centre climatopes are very densely built-up with massive and partly high-rise building volumes. You will often find this climatope in new city centres and in central business districts, such as La Defense in Paris or the Financial District in New York. There is hardly any vegetation in these areas, so the evaporation cooling is strongly reduced. All this leads to strong warming during the day and very limited cooling during the night, due to the strong heat retention of all these buildings.

Commercial district climatope

The commercial district climatope has similar characteristics as the city centre climatope when it comes to heat and wind effects, but on the metal roofs of the usually very massive buildings, you do see a clear cooling during the night. The streets and parking areas, however, do stay warm. This type of climatope is also assigned to similar areas with large, massive buildings, such as logistic centres and trade fair centres.

Industrial estate climatope

The industrial estate climatope has even more intensive heat characteristics than the business park climatope. During the day, residual heat from the production activities heats up these areas in addition to the solar radiation. If it's an area of continuous pro-duction, this effect continues throughout the night. The roofs cool down rather quickly here too, but the streets and enclosed areas for parking and logistics remain warm for a long time.

A railway yard climatope encompasses large, open areas of at least 50 metres wide. The gravel becomes really hot during the day, but because of the large sky view factor, it cools down more quickly during the night. These areas are, however, decidedly warmer than unsurfaced open areas. The large, open surfaces allow the wind to stream freely, which can help provide ventilation.

You can see from this list that the different climatopes cover all larger units of the city. A comprehensive citywide climatope map can be based on it. This climatope map, in turn, often forms the basis for further conclusions about wind patterns.

To make a climatope map of a city, you need information on land use, building structure, vegetation and surfacing. The government can oftentimes provide the required basic data. Many cities have these data in a Geographical Information System (GIS). To map the building density in districts, you need maps with the outlines of the buildings, but you also need to know the height of these buildings. Most municipalities have outline maps available, but not all of them have information on the building heights. Some cities have a municipal 'tree cadastre' with information about the vegetation. You can sometimes ask departments managing or

Railway yard climatope

Information and maps required for climatope classification

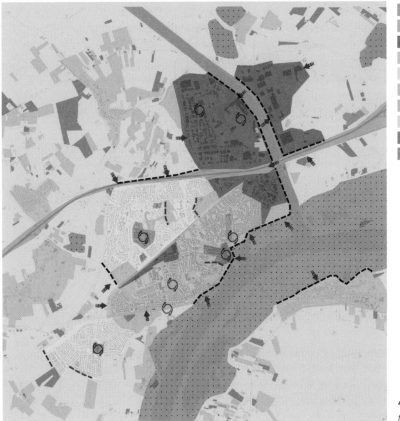

City centre
Infrastructure/railway yard
Industrial/commercial
City
Garden city
City periphery
Parks and fruit orchards
Open landscape
Forest and old orchards
Water
Highly dynamic area
Turbulence
Problem areas at south-western winds
Wind barrier
Potential wind during warm weather conditions

47 *Climatope map of Tiel, the Netherlands*

48 *Infrared photographs showing the surface temperatures in Arnhem, the Netherlands*

If this information is not available, you can also try to find maps indicating the surface temperature to find out what locations face heat-related problems. Remote sensing infrared maps, made with satellite images or special aerial photographs can provide insight into the surface temperature. These maps commonly show that some areas have a higher surface temperature than others. However, because these maps only depict the horizontal surfaces and not the vertical ones such as facades, which also retain much heat, you get a one-dimensional image. This image also does not show the air temperature. That's why these maps have only limited use, but they do sometimes suffice for a first indication of heat-related problems.

3.2   Indicating Wind Problems and Potentials

Research into typical seasonal wind directions and speeds

Before you can formulate design recommendations and meas-ures, you have to map the main wind situations of a city. Firstly, these are the situations with stronger wind, so as to characterize periods with wind nuisance. Secondly, this regards wind situations on very warm days, to identify possible cooling breezes. You can make wind roses for these two situations based on the weather data of weather stations close to the city. On cooler days, the wind usually has a different direction than on warm days. In many countries, the wind speeds on cool days are so high that they can lead to unpleasant situations in urban outdoor spaces. To prevent these situations, wind protection measures have to be taken. If the wind has a clear direction in warm situations, it is useful to design ventilation axes. If this is not the case, however, you should analyse potentials for inducing local wind systems.

Wind analysis maps of a city can show the areas with wind nuisance as well as the areas that can potentially provide ventilation. There are two typical areas with wind nuisance. Firstly, we experience wind nuisance in areas with much 'roughness', so with many buildings of strongly divergent volumes. In these areas, you can expect wind channelling, downwash and turbulence, causing the nuisance. Secondly, open areas within the city, such as large squares, very open park areas and riverfronts, often suffer from wind nuisance. This can interfere with recreational functions, and make it unpleasant or even difficult for people to walk or cycle.

*Localizing wind
nuisance areas*

The best way to map the potential for ventilation is to analyse the locations of 'warmer' and 'cooler' areas in the city. The larger the expected temperature gradients between warm and cooler areas, the stronger the airflows between these areas will be. These airflow potentials can come from coastal wind systems, be induced by differences in altitude or be based on temperature differences between climatopes.

*Finding ventilation
areas*

A topographical map will suffice to map potential coastal wind patterns. These patterns evolve on hot days without large-scale wind, when the city is already quite warm, for example during a heat wave. When there are no large obstacles like high-rise buildings or dunes in the coastal area of the city to deflect the wind, the coastal winds can provide cooling during the day. This cooling effect can fade at night, because the wind may then blow in the opposite direction. This depends on which area is actually warmer: the city or the sea. Meteorologists need to take specific measurements for each city to assess this. So oftentimes, a coastal wind can't provide cooling during the night. Other local airflows are usually more effective, for example urban winds or valley winds.

*Identifying coastal
wind areas*

To predict potential cold, nightly valley winds in cities with a clear relief, you need to consult detailed GIS or other detailed relief maps to look at the differences in altitude. Altitude differences over 50 metres mean there is a potential for these airflows. For these slow flowing downhill air movements to develop, the slopes need to be steep enough, at least 3 per cent; and there should be no obstacles like mounds, buildings or dense vegetation.

*Identifying valley
wind areas*

The temperature or climatope map is used to map the urban breezes caused by temperature gradients between warmer and cooler areas. We can expect significant temperature gradients particularly between areas with lower temperatures, such as open landscape or park, and densely built-up areas, such as city, city centre, and business and industrial estates. A breeze can form from the cooler to the warmer area – if there are no obstacles such as dikes, very dense vegetation or buildings at right angles to the breeze. The different wind potentials can then be mapped,

*Identifying urban
wind areas*

▥	Area with high potential for urban wind
▨	Area with low potential for urban wind
∿∿∿	Barriers for urban winds
→	Direction of urban wind
◉	Threat of wind nuisance

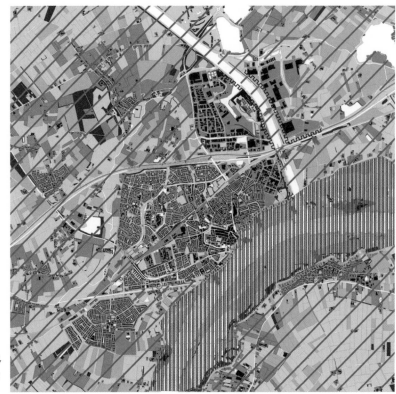

49 *Example of a wind map, showing urban wind areas: Tiel, the Netherlands*

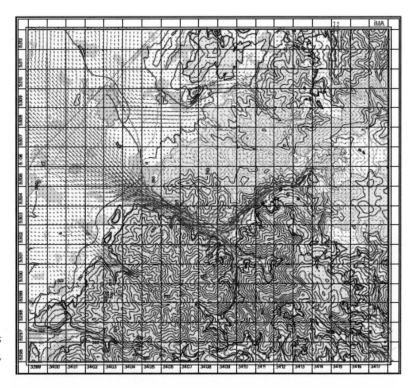

50 *Example of simulations of valley winds in Freiburg, Germany*

with indications of the expected flow speeds. This map should also show the obstacles for such airflows, because removing such obstacles can be an important measure to improve ventilation.

When a city has a complex morphology, for example because of big differences in altitude and many building volumes of different sizes, experts should simulate the wind systems with airflow simulations. These can be computer-generated simulations or wind tunnel simulations. Computer simulations can be used to represent flow patterns of thermally induced local wind systems such as coastal or valley wind systems. The results of these simulations can also be used to fine-tune wind analysis maps based on climatope maps.

Calculating local wind systems

3.3   Urban Climate Maps

With the methods described above to analyse the thermal and the wind situation, you can make quite accurate urban climate predictions for many cities. Non-meteorologists with some experience regarding the urban climate can often make these urban climate maps. Of course, these maps only offer qualitative information, not quantitative. This usually does not pose a problem, though, since the aim of these maps is not a meticulous scientific analysis, but to create a useful basis for design measures. These urban climate maps can show the information about the temperature and the wind separately (like for the municipality of Tiel, illustrations 47 and 49), or together in one single map (like the urban climate map of Arnhem, illustration 52). Cities built on a very complex terrain, for instance with a lot of relief *and* coastlines, have to be analysed by experts, who will make comprehensive urban climate maps. To determine whether experts need to be brought in, city planners or designers can consult with experts in the field of urban meteorology. Together, they can arrive at a good decision on the necessity of expert advice.

Urban climate maps summarize analyses

There are several expert systems that can depict the thermal component of the urban climate. Over the last couple of years, different types of software were developed to this end, usually based on GIS. German cities have been using these analysis-map systems for the urban climate already for decades in their urban planning practices. The city of Stuttgart has a remarkably long tradition of urban climate research, with urban meteorologists providing maps for the city. With their longstanding experience in the development of urban climate maps, German experts have developed heat maps for cities all over the world, such as Hong Kong and cities in Germany, the Netherlands, Taiwan, Vietnam and Brazil. Japan also has a long tradition of urban climate research. But a number of other European countries have also

Expert systems for urban climate maps

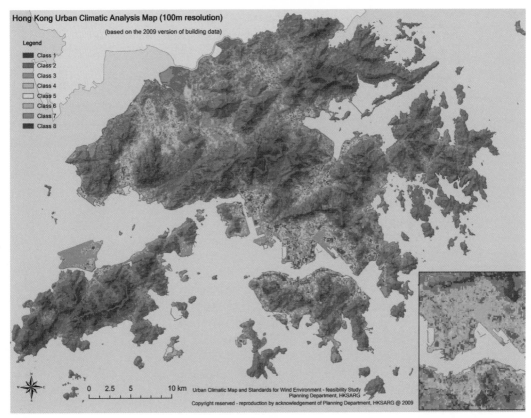

Hong Kong Urban Climatic Analysis Map (100m resolution)

(based on the 2009 version of building data)

Legend

- Class 1
- Class 2
- Class 3
- Class 4
- Class 5
- Class 6
- Class 7
- Class 8

0   2.5   5   10 km

51 *Urban heat map of
Hong Kong*

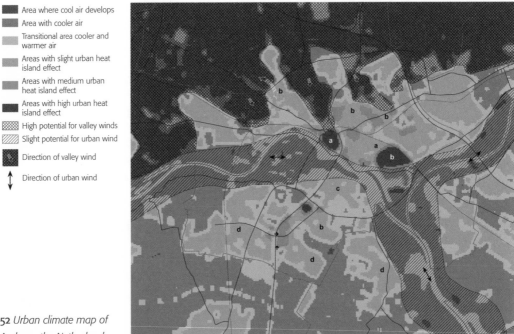

- Area where cool air develops
- Area with cooler air
- Transitional area cooler and warmer air
- Areas with slight urban heat island effect
- Areas with medium urban heat island effect
- Areas with high urban heat island effect
- High potential for valley winds
- Slight potential for urban wind
- Direction of valley wind
- Direction of urban wind

52 *Urban climate map of
Arnhem, the Netherlands*

made such urban climate maps, for example the United Kingdom, Switzerland, Sweden, Austria, Hungary and Greece. These maps are usually based on GIS and they show different parameter assessments (land use, topography, building heights et cetera), depicting qualitative information about the thermal and wind situation. The systems of the university of Kassel do not contain information about wind nuisance, as these always focus on heat and ventilation aspects. By now, some other cities have also started to map their urban climate with other expert systems.

The most reliable method for depicting the urban climate is taking long-term measurements in a close raster covering the whole city. In practice, this is very difficult to realize, so measurements are mostly used in combination with the mapping systems described earlier. Their function is then to substantiate information from the urban climate map systems with quantitative data. There are not many fixed weather stations in cities, so usually there is only a limited amount of meteorological data available. Installing and maintaining well-working weather stations can only be done occasionally; therefore this method isn't suitable to cover the entire urban area. In the Netherlands, the data of weather amateurs in cities have recently been used to gain insight into the urban climate. But these hobby weather

53 *The measurement-cargo bicycles of Wageningen University*

stations often are not located in the most significant districts or they're not optimally spread-out.

So urban meteorologist turn to other measuring methods, using a different way to systematically map the urban climate on important points of the city, namely mobile measurements. These follow meticulously plotted routes, crossing the areas most essential for the urban climate. These runs are repeated a number of times, especially during the most problematic times of the year (for instance during hot summer nights). The data gathered with these measurements can give an accurate account of the microclimatic conditions along the route, sometimes down to a mere few metres. Many cities have used cars that could also measure the other factors that are very important for thermal comfort, such as radiation and wind. In Canada and the Netherlands, specially equipped bicycles were used for these measurements. The advantage of bicycles is that they can also be used in areas inaccessible to cars, such as parks.

Measurements provide policymakers with 'hard facts'

Conducting these different measurements requires a lot of expert knowledge, resources and time, but it is often worthwhile. Experience teaches us that many policymakers often do not have enough confidence in the urban climate maps, because they do not offer 'hard facts and figures'. Even though such measurements often would not be necessary, because everyone with a little knowledge about the urban climate knows, for instance, that there are heat islands in every city. But politicians did not always believe urban heat islands existed, until the measured 'hard figures' made it abundantly clear that they do. So, you often need measurements to complement other analysis methods.

3.4   Vulnerability to Urban Climate Phenomena

Activities, health and age influence vulnerability

Before you start making large-scale plans and designs for the urban climate, you also have to assess the vulnerability aspect. Otherwise, you can't determine how urgent certain adaptation measures are. In the context of urban climate experience, the vulnerability obviously pertains to people. In this light, the most important aspects are how vulnerable different groups of people are to heat stress and wind nuisance, depending on their activities, age and health. You can usually show these vulnerability aspects in one map, with different layers for the different aspects. These aspects can then easily be taken in in the recommendations for adaptation.

Human activities take place in different time patterns, which have to be compared with the time patterns of the urban climate. Especially keep in mind that urban heat island effects are most prominent at night. These occur in several climatopes, but this does not always mean people are bothered by it. People living in

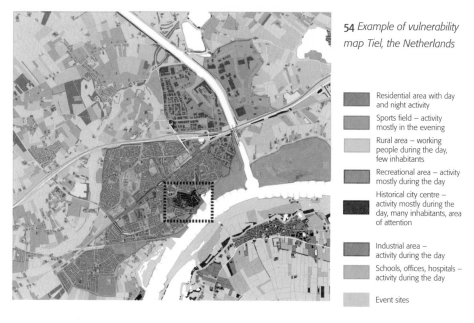

54 *Example of vulnerability map Tiel, the Netherlands*

Residential area with day and night activity

Sports field – activity mostly in the evening

Rural area – working people during the day, few inhabitants

Recreational area – activity mostly during the day

Historical city centre – activity mostly during the day, many inhabitants, area of attention

Industrial area – activity during the day

Schools, offices, hospitals – activity during the day

Event sites

densely built-up residential areas often have trouble sleeping at night because of the enhanced heat. But at a business park, also very hot at night, the heat does not bother anyone, because nobody's there at that time. There is much less urgency to adapt areas such as these. People do sometimes work nightshifts in industrial estates, but because these people work inside the buildings, which often have climate control, there is also usually less urgency for adaptation measures.

In a densely built-up city centre, with many people coming into the area to visit the shops, it *can* be very important to offer options for cooling during the day. The same could go for festival sites, where people can be exposed to strong heat on hot summer days.

Certain groups of people are particularly vulnerable to heat, especially young children, elderly people and people that are ill. Because these people spend a lot of their time in certain locations, such as day care centres, retirement homes or hospitals, these locations need to be mapped, since extra heat adaptation measures might be necessary.

Vulnerability to heat

Besides heat, wind nuisance is also a big problem in many cities. In areas where many people are outside, such as shopping streets, city squares or festival sites, it is very important to create a safe and comfortable wind climate. Therefore, areas with these activities should also be mapped and compared to the analyses of areas with wind nuisance.

Vulnerability to wind

4

Planning and Design for the Urban Climate at the City Scale

At the city scale, it is possible to significantly influence the urban climate, especially with measures affecting the air temperature and the ventilation patterns. The interventions concern larger parts of the city, such as making 'green wedges', 'landscape fingers', and assigning functions to areas that are to be developed in the future or that have to remain free of buildings. Some of the possible measures are scaled between the large and the micro scale, for instance which tree structures to use in parks, or how to keep ventilation axes open on the district level. So there are many possibilities for adapting the urban climate on a larger scale. These have to be made explicit, to provide urban designers and policymakers with concrete suggestions about what they can do in their own city to make it more 'urban climate proof'.

All the information derived from the urban climate analyses has to be weighed and translated into design measures and policy. Here, the interventions to lower the temperature are often different from those providing better ventilation for the city. The scale level of the measures to lower the air temperature is very diverse. These range from planting whole parks to the small-scale interventions that will be discussed in chapter 6. The ventilation measures are usually at a larger scale. The first part of this chapter is about various planning and design interventions for planners, landscape architects and urban developers. Of course, such measures then have to be actually implemented. This requires an adaptation to the existing policy instruments. The last section of this chapter offers insights on how to do this.

4.1   Reducing Heat Stress

The cool air plume reaches into adjacent areas

Most of the time, interventions aimed at preventing the city from overheating mean adding 'green'. This includes preserving and enlarging existing parks; and planning more small city parks, green wedges and green corridors. Several studies have demonstrated the cooling effect of large-scale green structures on their surroundings, and that this effect mostly depends on the size of these structures. The name for these green structures is very befitting: *park cool islands*. Swedish scientists measured a cooling effect of an impressive 6 °C up to 1100 metres from a large park in Gothenburg (150 hectares). A Canadian study indicated a cooling effect up to a hundred metres from neighbourhood parks on their leeside, on places where the wind could carry the cool air into adjacent streets. Even light wind can

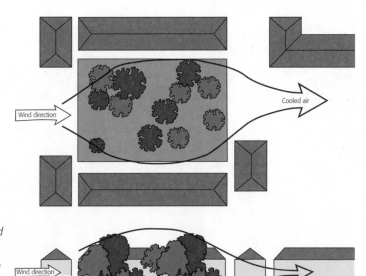

55 *'Plume of cool air' near a neighbourhood park with a ventilation corridor that has been kept open*

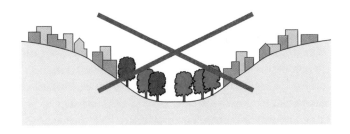

56 *Optimal distribution of green areas in a hilly terrain*

transport the cool park air like a 'plume of cool air' into the surrounding area, especially on the leeward side of the park. From this study, as well as from others, we can see how important it is not to over-build or -plant the ventilation areas for the cool air at the park edges.

Some urban meteorologists have also looked at the optimal size of parks and their distribution over the city. This resulted in the rule of thumb that city parks should be at least seven times as wide as the buildings that surround them. They also suggested that it is better to distribute several small parks over the densely built-up areas of the city than it is to build one large one. It also makes a difference where green areas are located in the relief of the city. If the green area is in a lower area than its surroundings, the heavier, cool park air can't get away; but if it is at a higher elevation than its surroundings, the cool airflow can stream downhill.

In light of the fact that parks with different vegetation also have different temperature patterns, it is important to look at these vegetation types in relation to the surrounding functions. If, for example, there are many people in the surroundings of a park during the day, as in city centres or office areas, cooling is more important at that time than it is at night. In daytime, parks with more trees offering shade provide better cooling than open parks with big lawns. It is therefore preferable in these locations to plant many trees in the parks. In a residential area, on the other hand, nightly cooling is very important. Open, green surfaces with a bigger sky view factor are more effective, because these areas cool down quickly at night and thus cool the surroundings. In an area with mixed functions, it is best to alternate open lawns and trees in a park. When the trees have high crowns and the cool air is free to flow around the trunks, a nice cooling effect can be

How to distribute green areas over the city?

Do we need parks for cooling during the day or at night?

73

expected. To ensure enough sunlight in all parks at wintertime, deciduous trees are always preferred.

Cooling a city with green areas, especially lawns, however, can face one 'bottleneck situation'. If there is not enough water available in the soil for the plants during a heat wave, the plants' evapotranspiration will be limited, as will their contribution to cooling. So especially during heat waves, you have to provide sufficient irrigation.

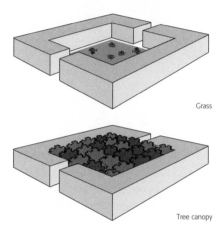

Grass

Tree canopy

57 *Parks with open lawns cool at night and parks with trees cool during the day*

Water bodies with dense plants can also provide cooling

Besides all types of green areas, water bodies can also provide cooling under certain circumstances. Generally speaking, water bodies are not very effective for cooling their surroundings, because they absorb much solar radiation during the day, which they give off during the night in the form of heat. Water bodies have a better cooling effect when they are densely grown with plants. The plants' shade keeps the water cooler, and by evaporating extra water through their stomata, they cool the air. Studies in Japan on the impact of rice paddies and in France of small ponds with a dense tree edge have shown these effects. We can expect the same effect for other combinations of water and plants, such as reed lands, alluvial forests and swamp forests.

Green and water recreation areas as 'heat refuges'

It can also help to create recreational areas at a short distance from the city for people to escape the heat. These areas should offer extra cooling through trees offering shade, water to swim in and possibly the use of local wind systems, for instance along river banks. These areas should be easy to reach by public transport and shaded bicycle paths.

Modifying the building and street structures to prevent warming

---

Besides the 'green' interventions for heat adaptation, there are also many adaptation possibilities in the built urban structure. For example, when parts of densely built-up areas are abandoned, they should not be built up anymore. New urban areas should be built with a lower building density. The heat emitted by buildings can easily linger in streets. In order to prevent this heat accumulation, it is best to design a more spacious H/W-ratio for streets or

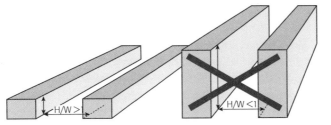

58 *Good and bad H/W-ratio in streets for preventing heat accumulation*

squares, so the heat can get away more easily. The balance of the street proportions should be examined carefully, so you do not unintentionally get wind nuisance (see section 2.2.3). In general, one can say that a height-width-ratio of 1:1, or narrower, retains much radiation and is not recommended. Moreover, the shadows of the buildings – large on our latitudes, most days of the year – often dominate for too many hours of the day in such narrow spaces, limiting the daylight intrusion of the buildings.

Changes in the functions of areas can also help solve heat problems, by changing these from a 'warm' into a 'cooler' climatope type. Many heat producing industrial estates, for example, might be converted into area types that produce less heat, such as commercial districts or even parks. Especially for abandoned industrial estates and brownfields, the latter is a very useful change in function. Where possible, large-scale traffic infrastructure can be reduced or converted into different functions. Alternatively, governments could implement more traffic control, like they do in London and Madrid, allowing fewer cars into the city and thus producing less anthropogenic heat.

Changing the functions of areas to cooler climatope types

4.2 Creating Ventilation Between and Within Districts

As discussed earlier, wind can sometimes be a problem, but it can also offer a potential for ventilation. Therefore, wind adaptation has two sides: on the one hand averting wind in areas prone to nuisance, and on the other hand inviting wind to come into areas with heat problems. The areas in the city with wind nuisance are usually relatively small-scaled. For the ventilation of the city, however, large-scale interventions are often more effective. These include a number of typical interventions, serving different purposes.

Depending on a city's topography, coastal wind systems might be used for daytime ventilation in coastal cities. At night, the coastal wind often brings warmer air into the city, which is not desirable in hot situations. If there are dunes between a coastal city and the coast itself, the soft coastal breeze usually can't reach the city. Experts should look into the exact interaction for each city. Generally speaking, though, the potential for coastal wind systems in temperate climate zones is relatively small.

**Ventilation axes
in valleys should
be kept open**

Valley wind systems that can transport cool air into the city at night should be facilitated. In order to do so, the high altitude areas generating the cool air and the downstream airflow lines should be kept open. This means the areas at higher altitudes ideally are not surfaced, built-on or forested. Otherwise, nightly radiation can't reach its maximum, and less cool air is produced or even none at all. Suitable land uses for these areas are arable land, pasture, heathland or similar landscape types. The areas through which the cool air flows down to the cities are usually steeper slopes and the bottom of the valley, because cold air flows down like water in a stream (also see illustration 50 with cold airflows in Freiburg, Germany). The speed with which the air flows is much lower than that of streaming water, though, and these soft, cool airflows are easily blocked. Because these airflows are so weak and the areas through which they stream are so small, these areas are very vulnerable. So these areas have to be protected in case they're still open. If these areas are already forested, built-on or blocked by other obstacles, removing these obstacles should be taken into consideration. When it's not possible to clear an airflow's entire path, the situation can be improved by arranging building or planting structures parallel to the direction of the flow, instead of at right angles to it (see illustration 59).

**Ventilation areas
between open land-
scapes and cities
should be kept open**

Urban winds, occurring between open areas (climatope 'open landscape') and climatopes generating much heat ('city', 'city centre', 'commercial district' and 'industrial estate' climatopes), can also be used for ventilation. Like the valley breezes, these

*59 Avoiding barriers
along contour lines in hilly
cities to allow for ventilation
and preferable building
configuration on the slopes*

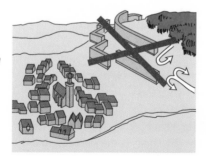
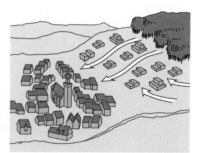
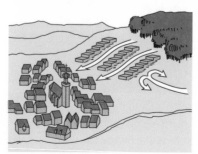
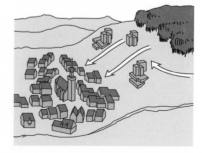

airflows are relatively slow and vulnerable to interception. Therefore, the possible ventilation courses between these areas should ideally be kept free of obstacles like earthen walls, buildings or many trees and shrubs.

To make optimal use of the effect of the temperature gradient between cooler and warmer climatopes, what works best is to make the gradient line between climatopes longer. This can mean 'open landscape fingers' or large green areas in a densely built-up city, ideally penetrating deep into the 'hot climatopes'. Few cities have such 'fingers' yet. To be able to realize them, cities should strategically open up these 'landscape fingers' when areas are restructured. These days, we have a promising opportunity to insert 'landscape finger systems' into areas with largely empty factory, business and office buildings. Part of the surfaced parking lots and such can become unpaved. The same can be done in abandoned terrains at the edges of 'hot climatopes'.

In these 'de-paved' areas, new functions like urban agriculture have great potential. It is important, however, to keep these areas relatively open, so as not to weaken their ventilation function. For planned urban expansions, it is recommendable to plan 'landscape fingers' penetrating into the city from the onset. This is the only way to ensure that ventilation axes are actually realized in the future urban structure.

60 *Avoiding barriers for urban wind between 'cooler' and 'warmer' climatopes*

Creating longer gradient lines between open landscapes and cities

Large green undeveloped areas can also produce urban wind

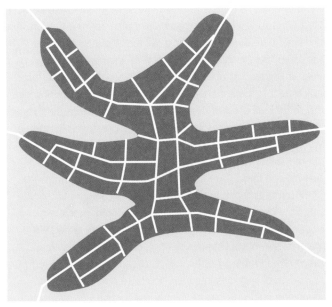

61 *Long gradients between cooler 'landscape fingers' and the densely built-up city offer much potential for ventilation*

 Built-up area

 Open area

4.3 Implementation in Planning Practices

*The 'recommen-
dations maps' for
urban planning*

It is possible to implement these recommendations for urban planning and design on the larger scale in various ways. Many German cities do so already. A 'recommendations map' is made based on the urban climate analyses maps or on climatope maps, with due consideration for areas that are extra vulnerable to heat stress amongst inhabitants. A recommendations map localizes diverse measures for urban climate adaptation. Typical recommendations on this map concern proposals on different scale levels: opening up ventilation corridors for urban winds, or opening up areas on slopes for downhill cold air systems. In the accompanying text, the general recommendations are usually supplemented with more precise information about possible small-scale interventions, such as green facades, trees and reflecting materials (see chapter 6). Most recommendations maps are 'paper' maps like the recommendations map for the Dutch city of Arnhem (see illustration 62 and compare with illustration 52). But since a few years, we see more digital and interactive systems as well. Large parts of the Ruhr area as well as the city of Stuttgart in Germany have had an extensive urban climate analysis done, resulting in a recommendations map available to everyone through a website on which the user can zoom into special themes and areas. Interactive maps are the latest development, for example with the MapTable system, on which stakeholders and experts can work on such a recommendations map together.

How the contents of these recommendations maps eventually get implemented in different countries varies a lot. In Germany, the information is translated on a large scale into a legally binding 'Flächennutzungsplan', an urban master plan defining the function of different areas. On a smaller scale, the information can be translated into the 'Bebauungsplan', a zoning plan. Illustration 63 gives an impression of local climate and recommendation maps indicating that the important ventilation zones into the city centre should be kept open or even that these should be cleared. Based on these maps, changes in existing zoning plans were made. For two cities in the United States and Canada, San Francisco and Toronto, urban climate analyses were made for the central districts, and these were translated into zoning plans, but these are absolute exceptions. Hong Kong uses the information from the urban climate maps in its urban planning for problematic areas. In the Netherlands, the information is partly used for the urban master plans ('structuurvisies'), and partly to test how 'urban climate friendly' new projects are. In Japan, the need for adaptation only comes into view on an 'ad hoc' basis. Then, adaptation guidelines are developed for this spot. Sometimes,

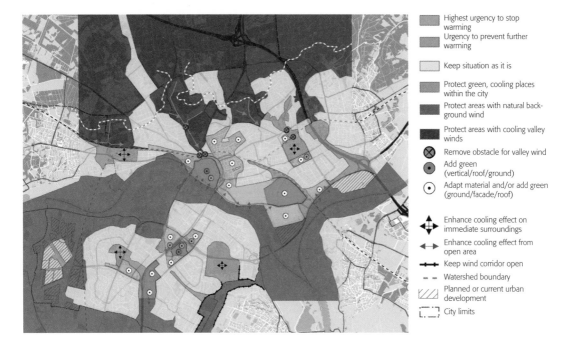

also special projects are realized to set an example for good adaptation practice. So, in these latter countries, projects do get tested, partly also through environmental assessments, and, usually small-scale, adjustments are made. This is not necessarily the most effective way to improve the urban climate. Larger interventions and legally binding implementation instruments are much more effective.

Here is an overview of implementation measures that can work within many urban planning systems, and the accompanying plans on different scale levels. These recommendations are based on the German implementation practice.

62 *Recommendations map Arnhem, the Netherlands*

Green fingers/wedges and large parks	Legally binding urban master plan
City and neighbourhood parks	Legally binding urban master plan
Changing functions of large, heat generating areas	Legally binding urban master plan
Lower building densities	Zoning plan
Lower H/W-ratio streets	Zoning plan
Orientation buildings to keep air flow paths clear	bestemmingsplan Zoning plan
Length of streets to prevent wind nuisance	Zoning plan

63 *Analysis and recommendation maps for valley winds, forming a basis for zoning plans, Stuttgart, Germany*

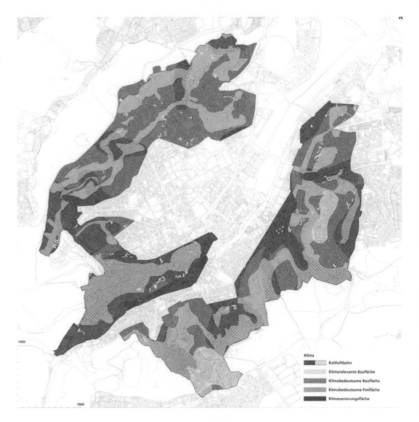

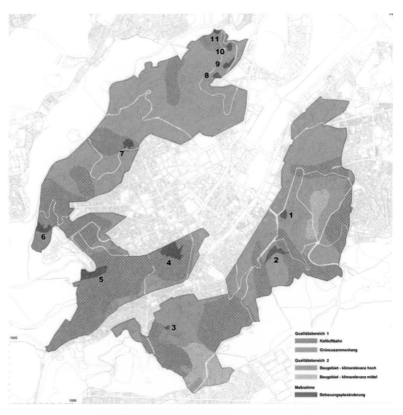

For large-scale interventions to improve the urban climate involving several municipalities in a (urban) region, the municipalities have to make solid agreements. The impact of a spatial intervention at the edge of one city, like building an industrial estate, can have a big impact on the heat climate of a neighbouring municipality. We should always keep in mind that the urban climate does not end at the city limits.

Other implemen-
tation options
can be imagined

5
Mapping the Microclimate

Adapting the microclimate sometimes means generally applicable 'no regret' interventions such as green facades, but for the most part these are site-specific measures playing into the local microclimate of an urban place or a neighbour-hood. On this small scale, analyses of the different characteristics of the local climate are therefore needed first, such as the sun exposures and wind patterns around buildings. If you do not map the microclimate before you start working on adaptation measures, you might choose the wrong solutions. For small-scale designs, solutions need to be tested during the design process often, and for this you need to know which analysis techniques are the most appropriate. The analyses entail diverse methods, partly pertaining to the physical aspects of the microclimate and partly to the psychological ones, but also combinations of both. Because the climate changes with the seasons, analyses usually have to be made at different times of the year. The patterns of use in each space often also play a role, and therefore these should be analysed as well. The analyses are generally depicted in maps, profiles and three-dimensional drawings, so they can be directly used for spatial design.

Depending on what is considered the most prominent problem for the microclimate at a certain location, a suitable analysis method should be selected. If, for example, a large-scale urban climate analysis (see section 3.3) indicates that wind and/or heat problems are to be expected, the local analysis can address this. But sometimes users' complaints about an uncomfortable microclimate can also give rise to a smaller scaled study, taking in the psychological factors as well. The following sections are about the different analysis methods; explaining for which issues these can be used, which data they will provide, how they work, what kind of expertise is needed and what you can expect in terms of manpower to conduct the analyses. Customarily, the physical factors come first, again subdivided into temperature and wind factors. It is also possible to map these physical factors integrally, with computer simulations and/or measurements. The analyses of the psychological aspects are next, and this chapter ends with a discussion of which analysis methods can complement each other in which situations.

5.1. Analyses of Physical Microclimate Experience

Analyses include microclimatic and spatial information

There are many ways to map the physical circumstances determining the microclimate experience in urban outdoor areas. In all cases, this means connecting urban climatic data with geographical data, in order to get a spatial representation of the urban climate aspects. People with a background in urban design and extra knowledge about the urban climate can carry out certain analysis methods. In part, these analyses are 'educated guesses'. The analyses are of a largely qualitative nature and 'rules of thumb', but in part, they can also be used to make quantitative estimations. For example, you can make approximate predictions about many wind patterns around objects or in open areas. Such general knowledge about the microclimate is often sufficient to make designs. Finally, a large number of factors have to be taken into account during the design process, and it is often unnecessary or even impossible to focus designs down to the smallest detail on the microclimate alone.

This chapter also features short descriptions of the specialist analysis techniques to provide some insight into the different methods for readers who act as commissioners for urban climate analyses. As a client, you can then use this basic knowledge to discuss with urban meteorology experts or urban physicists which analysis method is best suited for a certain project.

5.1.1 Shadow Simulations as Indicators of Temperature Experience

For mapping the thermal sensation, for example to indicate the optimal locations of sojourn places, the long- and shortwave radiation and the air temperature are most important. However, because the shortwave radiation in light and shadow has the largest impact on thermal sensation in our parts of the world, it usually suffices to simulate sun and shadow patterns, for instance with common 3D-software such as AutoCAD and SketchUp. Beforehand, you have to carefully consider which shadow situation you are analysing: is it a place used in winter (when shadows are very long) or in summer (when shadow patterns are much shorter), and what kind of use are you designing for? The shadow simulation then has to take those situations into account.

With shadow simulations, you can make accurate maps that also include information about solar radiation and emissivity

It is also possible to generate an image of the shadow patterns for a longer period of time, say over the course of a whole year. In order to do so, you have to simulate the shadow patterns of 21 June and 22 December. These two dates are the longest and the shortest day of the year, depending on the location on either the Northern or the Southern Hemisphere. Because these are the extremes, they also cover all patterns in between (see illustration 64). Using these, you can make a more in-depth analysis.

You can, for example, see what percentage of the time a spot is continuously shaded or is exposed to the sun. You can easily make a graphical representation by projecting the shadow patterns for different seasons on top of each other, using a program such as Photoshop. The overlap automatically shows how much shortwave radiation comes into a certain location. With this, you can make a rough estimation of the heat absorption, and thus indirectly also the possible radiation. When heat problems are to be expected at such places, specific measures can be taken. For example: if street profiles need to be 'cooler', it is helpful to make such an analysis for these streets. In the example (illustration 65) you can see which shadow patterns occur in streets with different H/W-ratios with a north-south and an east-west orientation. The lines in these profiles show which places receive too much sun, thus where to expect heat problems.

You can quickly make shadow analyses with common design programs

Such shadow simulations can usually be made quickly, because in many design projects, the geometrical information is already generated in a three-dimensional design program. Then it's very easy to make the simulations for different points of time. You do not need any knowledge about the urban climate, and you do not need to consult any experts. On the other hand, the simulations do not offer precise information about albedos and emissivity of materials. To calculate these, expert simulation software, for instance Rayman is used; but this software is not

Pros and cons of shadow simulations

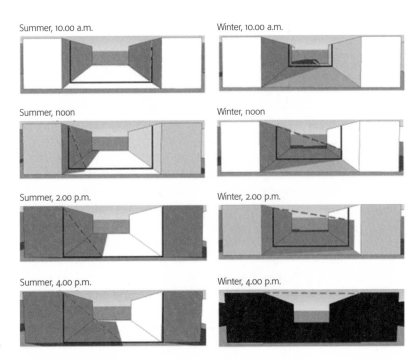

Summer, 10.00 a.m.

Winter, 10.00 a.m.

Summer, noon

Winter, noon

Summer, 2.00 p.m.

Winter, 2.00 p.m.

Summer, 4.00 p.m.

Winter, 4.00 p.m.

64 *Series of shadow patterns in a street profile*

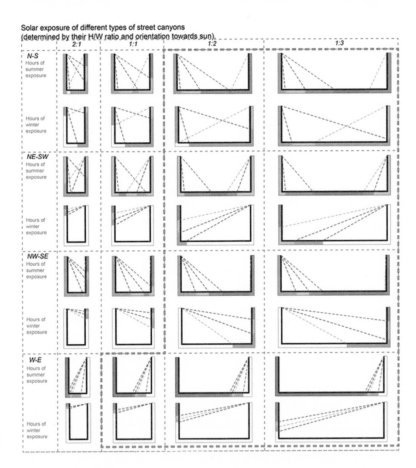

Solar exposure of different types of street canyons
(determined by their H/W ratio and orientation towards sun).

	2:1	1:1	1:2	1:3
N-S Hours of summer exposure				
Hours of winter exposure				
NE-SW Hours of summer exposure				
Hours of winter exposure				
NW-SE Hours of summer exposure				
Hours of winter exposure				
W-E Hours of summer exposure				
Hours of winter exposure				

65 *Matrix of shadow simulations with sunshine percentages for different street profiles with varying orientations, plus indications of where heat problems are to be expected (red dotted line)*

used regularly, since it does not reflect other factors important for the experience of the microclimate, such as wind and air temperature.

5.1.2   Educated Guesses about Wind Patterns

For knowledge about wind patterns, for example to allocate pedestrian or bicycle routes or sojourn places, rough estimations of wind patterns can be helpful. Especially during the design process itself it is practical to have such estimations at your disposal to make quick decisions about design alternatives. With the knowledge from section 2.2.3 you can draw many conclusions about the wind situation in a certain urban setting. The effects of design interventions can also be assessed. It is possible to analyse, for example, the wind flow patterns around the buildings, through drawing in a map, profile or perspective drawing (see illustration 66).

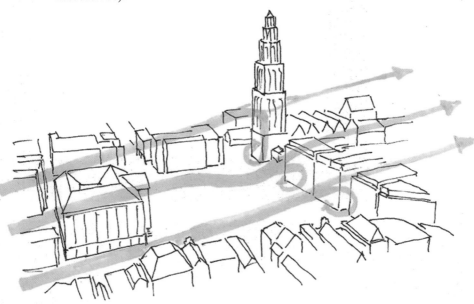

It is also possible to sketch the places with higher wind speeds caused by corner streams and their size for an existing situation or for a design proposal.

But you can also make approximate projections of rough patterns of where there is shelter from the wind, based on the patterns discussed in chapter 2. The example in illustration 67 shows a pattern of high hedges, projected as wind protection on a square of 100 x 100 metres. The hedge pattern is distributed in such a way that virtually the entire square is protected from the wind.

Such educated guesses about wind patterns do not necessarily have to be made by urban meteorologists, since a good basic knowledge of wind dynamics will often suffice. Besides, it is much

66 Example of estimated wind patterns on the Grote Markt, Groningen, the Netherlands

Pros and cons of educated guesses for wind

67 *Example square of*
100 x 100 metres with
wind protection hedges
and sheltered areas

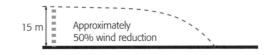

15 m | Approximately
50% wind reduction

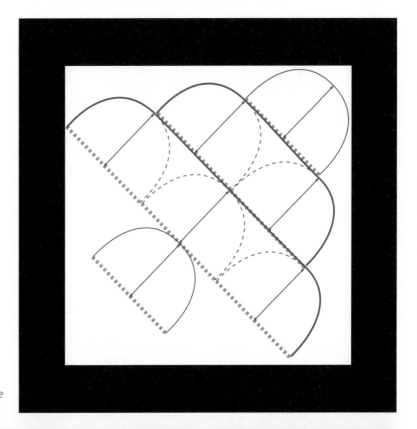

68 *A model of a city in the*
wind tunnel

cheaper and faster than hiring specialists. The potential of these educated guesses are often underestimated, especially their important role in the beginning of the design process when many rough estimates have to be made and weighed against each other. On the other hand, educated guesses are obviously less reliable and accurate than the work of specialists described above. In that case, experts, such as meteorologists or urban physicists have to make more accurate analyses based on simulations and measurements.

5.1.3 Wind Tunnel Tests

Wind flow tests in wind tunnels are done when it is important to have accurate predictions on future wind patterns, or to simulate an existing microclimate situation of a location where you can't take measurements, for instance. Wind tunnel experiments are often used in projects requiring an assessment of the impact of a high-rise building. One of the important effects is how tall buildings affect wind patterns, which can lead to wind danger and nuisance. But these wind tunnel tests are also sometimes done when designers, municipalities or property developers expect wind problems at the pedestrian level. Some countries use technical standards to counter wind nuisance in outdoor spaces, for instance the Dutch NEN8100 standard. A wind tunnel test can also be part of an environmental impact assessment for large new buildings. But many countries simply do not have these kinds of regulations. Then it comes down to a municipality or builder to have wind tunnel tests done, for example to prevent future damage claims.

When do we use wind tunnel tests?

In a wind tunnel, airflows are generated and directed to scale models of areas or buildings in controlled circumstances. This way, one can determine the effect of the wind on the area or on objects, and, vice versa, that of the area on the redistribution of airflows. These wind experiments can simulate all kinds of wind situations. In the wind tunnel, you can set different wind directions, ideally representing the most important wind situations. You can also simulate different wind speeds and in some wind tunnels even gusts. This way, wind effects on buildings and people can be determined. A model for a wind tunnel experiment should always represent a larger area than the area you are studying. This is to make sure you include the considerable influence of surrounding volumes.

What happens in a wind tunnel?

The wind speeds on relevant spots of the model are then shown in different ways for a number of important wind directions and wind speeds. This can be done in several ways. Smoke can be injected in the airflow on certain spots, so you can see eddies around the object. Alternatively, lightweight threads can be glued to the surface of the object, especially in places considered to be of crucial interest for the study, for instance at

In wind tunnel tests, what is measured where?

69 *Smoke simulations in the wind tunnel of Colorado State University*

the pedestrian level or in locations where people will repose. The movement of the threads fluttering in the wind highlights local wind speed differences and eddies. Another method is to install small, electronic or mechanical measurement modules on or close to the scale model. Blowing light sand into the model can also show whirl patterns. In spots with much wind, the sand will be blown away, to settle on sheltered spots.

Pros and cons of wind tunnel tests

The predictions made with wind tunnel experiments are very reliable. The experiments are independent of weather situations, because they take place under completely controlled circumstances and many different situations can be simulated. Just like with outdoor measurement points, wind tunnel measuring points cannot be installed in all places of a scale model, so there will always be 'holes' in the spatial distribution of measurements. But the density of measuring points in wind tunnels can always be higher than that of measurements actually done outside in the cities themselves.

Wind tunnel experiments are very specialist work and there are only a few wind tunnels. Some of the wind tunnels and experts can be found in universities and some at private consultancies. Therefore, wind tunnel tests are usually quite costly.

5.1.4   Computer Wind Simulations

When do we use wind simulations?

Computer wind simulations can essentially be used for the same purposes as wind tunnel tests, so these computer simulations are used as an alternative for the wind tunnel tests for impact assessments and such.

Wind simulations can usually depict the wind flows in a relatively high resolution. These computer simulations calculate the wind's flow patterns and its speed, and represent it in four dimensions: the three spatial dimensions plus time. In jargon these analyses are called 'Computational Fluid Dynamics' (CFD) simulations and they're also used for other flow-related calculations, such as water flows. There are several CFD-simulations programs, and for simulating urban contexts 'Fluent' is quite common. It is preferable to leave the appropriate software choice up to the experts. The grid sizes of these simulations can be very diverse, depending on the expected size of flow patterns. The patterns essentially have the same shape on all scale levels, but are simply smaller or larger in scale. It is best to include a large part of the surroundings in the simulations, since the surroundings are of great influence on the wind patterns. But the grid should not be too fine, because most computers do not have the capacity to make such complex calculations. So you should always consider the size of the area you want to do calculations on, the mesh width of the grid and the available computing power. The simulation results usually show both the wind's direction and its speed on different locations. The wind direction is generally indicated with arrows, and the wind speed through the thickness of these arrows or by colour coding. Some software can show these patterns in videos, but that requires very strong computer processors.

Computer wind simulations provide a lot of flexibility and can represent many different situations, but there are many bottlenecks. Firstly, the CFD-simulations are less accurate than wind tunnel tests. Secondly, there are sometimes problems with how much time computer processors need. When, for example, you need a very detailed simulation of a larger area (thus with a fine grid), many data have to be calculated, often too many for most computers. So you then have to buy computers with fast processors and a lot of memory, or you have to pay for the use

How do computer wind simulations work?

Pros and cons of computer wind simulations

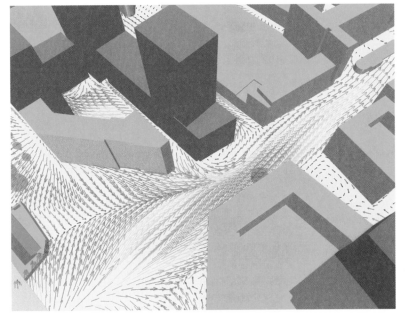

70 *CFD-wind simulations for a project in The Hague, the Netherlands*

of external supercomputers. Both solutions are very expensive. Add to this that you need experienced specialists to work with the software. So it is a somewhat costly analysis method.

5.1.5 Computer Simulations for Combined Microclimate Phenomena

When to use integrated computer simulations for micro- climate phenomena?

Computer simulations integrally showing all microclimatic phenomena are needed when it is not possible to take measurements, or when a design has to be tested before it is built. Computer simulations can represent long time sequences of, for instance, several weeks. On many 'real' locations, such longitudinal measurement campaigns are not an option. Because computer processors' power can easily become a limiting factor, you have to carefully consider which time sequences have to be simulated for which locations. At the moment, there is only one type of software that simulates and maps all physical factors of microclimate experience: Envi-met®.

How do integrated simulations work?

Envi-met® works with a three-dimensional grid, in which a spatial situation is 'built'. The user can determine the mesh of that grid, so it can show larger contiguous areas. These computer simulations depict the physical parameters of microclimate experience in four dimensions: the three spatial dimensions plus time. You can also use this software to compare different simulations, and map the differences.

I will illustrate this with examples of Envi-met®-simulations I made of the Spuiplein in The Hague in the Netherlands. For reference, the existing situation was simulated first. Subsequently, several design alternatives to improve the microclimate were simulated. To determine which alternative was best, I compared the simulations of the existing situation with those of the design alternatives, both for a cool autumn day, when most microclimatic problems were expected. I then looked at the improvement or deterioration of the microclimate in the new situation, using the 'difference' function. The comparative map (illustration 71) shows many green areas, which means that the design interventions improve the microclimate in these areas.

Pros and cons of integrated computer simulations

Because Envi-met® can be used to simulate the microclimate independent of external circumstances, it is very flexible. Contrary to in situ measurements, where you can only take measurements in a limited number of places, computer simulations can reflect on the microclimate of a much larger area. Moreover, these simulations can be used to estimate what non-existent micro- climatic situations will be like. Consequently, the role of these integrated simulations in spatial design processes can be very valuable.

But whether or not simulations can be used in design processes calls for careful consideration, because there are a few bottlenecks. The first one is the mesh or resolution of the

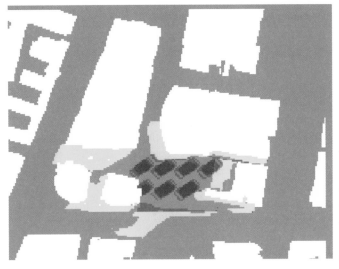

71 *Envi-met®-simulation for the Spuiplein in The Hague, the Netherlands, comparison of the existing situation with a design (combination of wind-screen and shadow trees)*

software. For example: if you need a very detailed simulation (so with a fine mesh) of a larger area, exponentially more data have to be calculated. The program can't always handle this and stops working. The second bottleneck often is the computer processors. If their memory space is insufficient, they can take a very long time to make the calculations or even crash. To prevent this, you have to invest in computers with a fast processor and a lot of memory. This will drive up the costs of the project. Another problem is that some parts of the software are not yet properly developed and calibrated. This means that the results of the simulations have not been sufficiently compared to real situations, so these results are partly hypothetical. Only experienced experts can assess the predictive value of these simulation results. These experts and the required computing power make the production of good simulations relatively expensive.

The long computing time can slow down design processes. Design alternatives first have to be 'calculated' before new steps can be taken. This can be disruptive for the progress of projects. For the future, we can expect fewer computing power issues, because computers keep getting faster. Also, the calibration of Envi-met® is continuously improved, especially in the latest version, and thus its simulations become increasingly reliable.

5.1.6 Measurements of all Microclimate Phenomena

Measurements are a very precise and reliable way to analyse the urban climate. In some cases, measurements have to be done to provide 'hard facts', for instance to have reliable evidence to support implementation of adaptation measures. Logistically, however, measurements can often be complicated, so they have to be well prepared. The main question before you start commissioning series of measurements: what situation should

In which cases do you use measurements?

the measurements reflect? Does it concern, for example, an area where you can expect many heat-related problems in summer? Then the measurements should be conducted when the heat problems are biggest. Or does it concern an area of public space with wind nuisance? Or do you want to know what the microclimate is like throughout the year? Then it is important to do measurements in different seasons. In all cases, it is crucial that measurements are conducted on several days and at different times of the day. One single measurement does not tell you very much, because it can only give you a random indication of the situation at that moment in time and is very probably not representative of the general situation or the situation you want to study. Longitudinal studies are the most reliable.

What is measured where?

Ideally, series of measurements include all physical parameters of microclimate experience: air temperature, relative humidity, short- and longwave radiation, and wind speed and wind direction. From these, thermal comfort indices can be derived (see chapter 1). If you only want to map heat problems, measurements should be conducted on hot days and especially at night, when the urban heat island is most prominent. In some countries, where warm or problematic situations often come with a typical wind (such as the Chinook and the Föhn wind), such wind flows should also be considered. If in certain places valley or urban winds are to be expected, it is also advisable to measure the wind in these places. To show wind problems, it can be sufficient to only measure wind speed and direction. But because people's thermal comfort usually depends on wind and other parameters, it is better to include radiation and air temperature as well.

The spots for measurements should be chosen strategically, so they reflect typical microclimate situations at different points in time. When measurements are taken in a street, this ideally should be done on both sides of the street (the sunny side and

72 *GIS-maps with data of the Spuiplein in The Hague, including air temperature and wind directions*

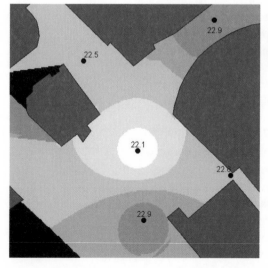
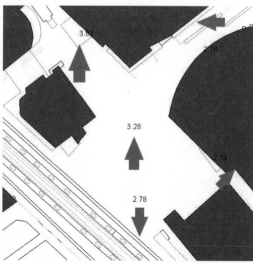

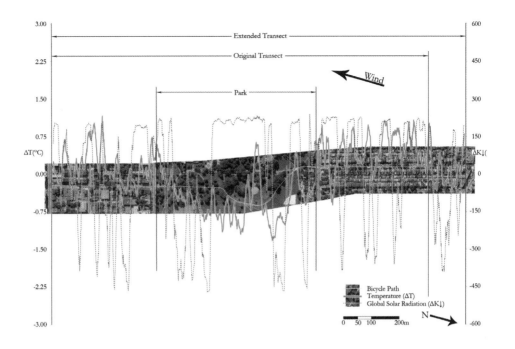

73 *Measurement transects in Toronto with differences in air temperature (red) and solar radiation (blue)*

the shaded side), but also on the corners (because of the different wind patterns). In a garden or a square, the typically sunny or shaded spots should also be taken into account, as well as the windy spots and the sheltered ones. For measurements inside houses or on facades, the sun's orientation and the wind exposure should be kept in mind. So, there are many different types of measurements. Here are some examples to clarify these.

Some of my own research was in response to the fact that many people complained about an uncomfortable microclimate on Dutch city squares. I therefore studied microclimate experience on squares in several cities. The focus was on mapping possible heat and wind problems on these squares. In order to do so, I made daytime measurements several times a day during the course of the outdoor seasons spring through autumn. On a number of fixed spots on the squares, I measured the air temperature, humidity, radiation, wind speed and direction. These spots were mainly chosen based on the sun and shadow situation and the wind patterns. The spots had to represent the relevant different microclimate situations: very sunny spots and spots with much shadow; spots that were very exposed to the wind and spots that were sheltered from it most of the time. This was to ensure we did not get a biased view of the general microclimate situation. The data were presented in GIS.

Examples of measurements on Dutch squares

In Toronto, scientists focussed a series of measurements on the heat aspect in residential areas and on the question of how small parks can help cool these neighbourhoods. The aim was to gain a better insight into the cooling impact of the neighbourhood parks, and especially in how far the parks' cooling reached into

Examples of measurements in Toronto, Canada

the surrounding residential areas. They used a specially equipped bicycle to ride through the parks and the surrounding neighbourhoods. To make a 'temperature profile' reflecting the differences between the parks and the neighbourhoods, the scientists chose routes crossing these areas in transects

Measurements result in reliable data and 'hard facts'. This is supportive in decision-making processes to implement urban climate adaptation interventions. On the other hand, series of measurements require a lot of expensive expert manpower and expensive equipment. Fixed measuring equipment has to be placed in safe spots and it has to be vandalism proof. It also is not possible to place the equipment everywhere you would like, so often you can't collect data in the desired spatial distribution. Moreover, it takes a lot of time to do measurements, and they also depend on the unpredictability of the weather. In the unlucky event that a whole year passes without the relevant climate phenomena you want to measure, you have no choice but to extend the measuring period. This makes it hard to plan series of measurements. Another disadvantage is that measurements only reflect existing situations; they do not offer insights on future interventions. And it is this type of information that is crucial for design proposals for spatial planning in cities. In that case, simulations are in order to predict future situations.

5.2 Mapping Psychological Aspects of Microclimate Experience

The analysis of the physical microclimate does not cover all aspects of microclimate experience. As we know, psychological aspects are important as well. People associate certain colours and materials with 'warm' or 'cool' microclimates, even if these do not necessarily have any influence on the physical microclimate. People also associate certain spatial configurations with a typical microclimate, even if they don't know much about the laws of physics behind them. Therefore, an environmental psychological approach is a vital part of microclimate analyses. The results offer a lot of relevant information for spatial designers.

Finally, spatial designs are largely aimed at people's experience of a place, and not just the physical reality of it. All methods mapping the psychological aspects of microclimate experience can be used to study existing spatial situations, and in the case of small redevelopments that do not have too much impact on the spatial structure. These methods are not suitable for projects in which completely new urban environments are developed.

5.2.1 Mental Maps

When you need to link several aspects of microclimate experience directly to certain spaces, a *mental map* method can be useful. Such a mental map can reveal on which locations in an area people perceive certain microclimates. The results of mental mapping methods can be useful when smaller urban places are refurbished, and especially when the aim is to improve microclimate perceptions. Therefore, several European countries are starting to use these methods.

To make mental maps, you conduct interviews with users of urban outdoor spaces. Respondents indicate what their long-term experience is with for example sun and shadow, wind and rain, and on which specific locations they experienced these conditions. With this information, you can make an individual mental map (see illustration 74). Preferably, these interviews are done on location, so the respondents can point out the areas they link to certain microclimate characteristics. Individual people usually don't know every spot in the study area, for example because their daily routines only cover certain routes. So individual mental maps often do have white spots. But if you ask a sufficient number of people about their mental maps, you usually do obtain a complete image.

The results of all individual mental maps are then overlapped. The easiest way to do this is through GIS. The result is a 'collective' mental map of the microclimate (see illustration 75). In these maps you can use colours or numbers to indicate how many people labelled certain spots with certain microclimate characteristics.

In my own research I have found the information from the collective mental maps often tally well with the measured reality. So it is a reasonably reliable analysis method. You can make these mental maps without much knowledge of urban meteorology. You do need to have some interview and GIS

When do you use mental map methods?

How do you make mental maps for the microclimate?

Pros and cons of mental maps

74 *Example of an individual mental map of the Neckerspoel area in the Dutch city of Eindhoven*

experience. If you don't have this experience yourself, you can consult with social science or environmental psychology specialists. Since the subject of analysis is people's long-term experience, independent of the current situation, you can use this mental map method any time you like.

Moreover, several interviewers can interview people about their experience simultaneously. So this method is relatively fast and inexpensive. The data-analysis does take some time, but certainly less than extensive measurements or simulations, which are more costly as well. Yet, these mental maps are based on non-expert knowledge, which might be coloured by other factors. Sometimes, places get a certain 'microclimate label' because they are avoided for social reasons, or because they are loved for their cosy ambiance, even though these labels have nothing to do with the micro-weather in the city. Therefore we do have to be careful when interpreting the results.

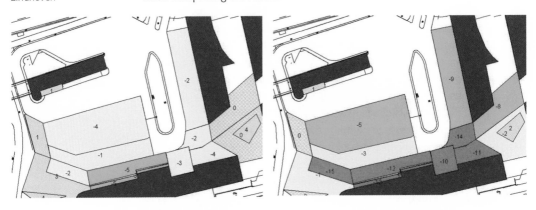

75 Example of collective mental maps for sun/ shade (left) and wind (right), Neckerspoel, Eindhoven

5.2.2   Interviews

When do you use interviews for analysis?

When you want to know about people's general microclimate experience in a city's outdoor area, interviews can offer relevant information. The need for systematic interviews may arise, for example, when people express vague complaints about the ambiance and/or microclimate of an area, as we often see on websites and blogs. Interviewing users can reveal the problems behind these complaints. Interviews usually do not depend on a certain time, so you can basically use this method throughout the year.

The main questions concern the relationship of microclimate experience and all factors you can influence through urban design, such as size, scale, openness, proportions, colours and materials used. It is advisable to ask about these aspects in interviews. You can also analyse which specific user groups have certain experiences or behaviours. People from different generations or cultural backgrounds for example, experience the microclimate differently. Interview results can offer valuable information about target groups of a spatial design for the microclimate. A conclusion from such interviews could be, for instance, that you should create more places with a very mild microclimate for elderly people to enjoy. Or such an analysis might show the need for more shaded places for picnickers. Many other results are possible, of course.

The information obtained through interviews is normally not as clearly linked to specific locations as the information in mental map analyses. But in some cases this more general information can be translated into a spatial representation. In two of my Dutch studies, for instance, I translated interview results about the perception of materials into maps of urban spaces. I asked people which materials in the study-area had a 'cold' or 'warm' appearance in their opinion. I then localized these materials in the area, so I could make a map from this information. In the 'materials experience map' of the Spuiplein in The Hague, for example, people labelled the present materials as very 'cold'. The 'materials experience map' of the Grote Markt in the city of Groningen, on the other hand, shows that people consider the materials in that place to be much 'warmer'.

What information can you get from interviews?

Because urban design is essentially aimed at people and their experiential and behavioural patterns, these interview results yield relevant knowledge for designers, especially if this information can be translated into maps. In a relatively short time, interview studies can gather a wealth of information, so this is a relatively inexpensive and fast way to collect reliable basic information. People with some experience in interview techniques can conduct these interviews. If you don't have interview experience yourself, you can also hire experience research specialists. Keep in mind, however, that people's experiences do not always match with a measurable reality. This can sometimes lead to quite dangerous situations when people misjudge their microclimatic surroundings. For example: people often don't

Pros and cons of interviews

76 *'Material experience maps' of the Spuiplein, The Hague and the Grote Markt, Groningen, the Netherlands*

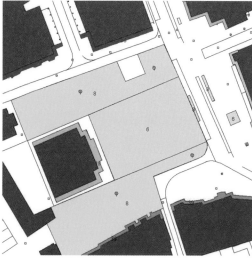

realize that in some places gusts can be so strong that they can cause accidents. Also when it comes to heat and sun, people don't always notice the threat of serious dehydration or damaging ultraviolet radiation, as you can see from the number of people with very unhealthy sunbathing habits. In cases where you can expect these types of serious microclimate problems, it is better to also use physical analysis methods. This way, you can put people's subjective estimations into a more 'objective' context.

5.2.3   Observations

When do you use observations as an analysis method?

Sometimes people can't talk about their experiences, because they are not aware of them or because they can't express themselves very well verbally (think of children, foreigners or people with certain disabilities). You can then use observations as an analysis method. This can be a useful option when, for example, small interventions are needed to improve the microclimate in urban spaces. For precise localization of interventions, observations can indicate where you will find many people and subsequently if they either seek out or avoid certain microclimatic circumstances. The design interventions can then address these specific circumstances and locations.

Making observations and mapping them

Observing people's behaviour can offer information about local microclimate experiences without people having to talk about it explicitly. You make these observations on location at different times or in different seasons to map behavioural patterns. There are several indicators for behavioural changes related to the microclimate. When people experience certain situations as either comfortable or uncomfortable, they first change the way they dress, for example by taking off their coat or by putting it on. If this is not enough, people change locations. They find a place in the sun or in the shadow, out of the wind or one that is nice and breezy when it's hot. The spatial configurations of places that people seek out in these cases can subsequently be categorized according to the typical microclimatic characteristics. These microclimatic characteristics can then be adapted through design interventions in places where needed. To make an observations map with sufficient informational value, you have to observe a larger area in its totality, such as an entire square or street. Otherwise, you can't get a good view of people's spatial movement patterns. To be able to compare results, you need an overview of the complete spatial patterns of sojourn and movement at the same points in time. Therefore, it works best when observers choose a spot in the middle of a space or another strategic place from where they can have a good overview. If this is not possible, more people can make observations from different spots onsite. The observation maps can represent the places where people are stationary (see illustration 77 for the city of Kassel), but you can also add

77 *Observations maps of stationary presence in Kassel, Germany.*

information about people's movements (see illustration 78 for the city of Groningen).

You do not have to be an expert to make these observations. Making observations and mapping them is therefore a relatively simple method to analyse the way people react to the microclimate. Since this does not normally require specialists, it is also a relatively inexpensive method. Getting the information you need, can sometimes take a long time, because you have to make observations in different seasons or you have to wait for specific weather circumstances. Moreover, people's spatial behavioural patterns depend on many other factors besides the microclimate. Oftentimes the fact that someone is at a certain location or takes a certain route for a purely functional reason, such as an appointment or taking the shortest route, is much more important than consciously choosing to be in a specific microclimate. The results of these observations can therefore only be reliable in combination with other analysis methods, such as simulations.

Pros and cons of observations

78 *Observations maps with stationary and movement patterns, Grote Markt, Groningen, the Netherlands*

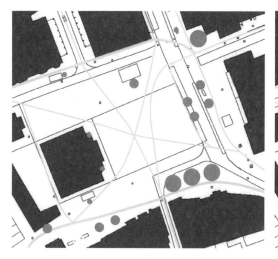
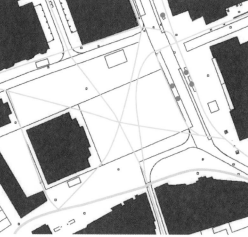

5.3   Combinations of Analysis Techniques

*Use simulations
and wind tunnel
tests for new
development projects*

As we have seen before, it is sometimes best to combine analysis methods. Depending on the aim of the analyses, certain analysis combinations make more sense than others. An important question is: are the analyses used to support a completely new development project or are they intended for small interventions in an existing space? In the first case you can only use simulation methods, since these can reflect a non-existing situation. If you need to know about wind, a combination of wind simulations and wind tunnel tests is ideal. The wind simulations can then be compared to the wind tunnel results, thus adding to the reliability of the results. There are more options when projects involve smaller interventions in existing situations, for example placing new surfacing, furniture or adding some trees. You can then use all described analysis techniques.

In general, it is advisable to combine simulations or measurements with experience/behaviour research. In this way you make sure that you map the physical *and* the psychological aspects of spatial microclimate experience. These methods do, however, often require lengthy in situ studies. The measurements and simulations are often costly, as they involve much specialist work.

*Use mixed analysis
techniques for rede-
velopment projects*

If these extensive and expensive analyses are not an option, then combining simulations with mental maps and/or interviews can be an alternative. The simulations generate a model of the physical circumstances. These can then be compared to the results from the mental maps or the interviews. This combination of analyses is less time-consuming and more flexible when it comes to the time in which the study is conducted.

6
Designing for Microclimate Experience

To make the urban climate more comfortable, many adjustments are needed, especially on the small scale – because many small interventions can have cumulative effects. There are many small-scale design solutions to improve all aspects of microclimate experience. Think of many 'green' landscape architectural interventions; urban design solutions such as configuring buildings and open spaces; and finally solutions in the field of public design – the refurbishment of public space. There are many traditional solutions that used to be applied in cities, landscapes and gardens, but that have since been forgotten. I will put these in the spotlight once again. But there are many new solutions as well, as will be illustrated with examples from various countries in the temperate climate zone. When it comes to multifunctional adaptation measures, inspiring examples will show there is much room for innovation. We can use all these small-scale interventions to improve the local microclimate. This will lead to authentic, location-specific designs for spaces and neighbourhoods.

After you have made suitable analyses of a microclimatic environment and identified problems and potentials, you can make location-specific designs. This chapter offers a broad overview of various small-scale adaptation interventions in a fact-sheet catalogue at the end of this chapter. You will also find a complete overview on the back flap of this book. Again, the design measures in this chapter are described in the same order as elsewhere in this book: temperature experience first, wind experience second and psychological aspects last. Protection from rain in outdoor areas is an extra theme in this chapter. New, multifunctional solutions are also discussed, influencing several factors of the microclimate. Many of the solutions discussed here have one main purpose. A canopy, for example, only blocks solar radiation. Measures against wind or for ventilation usually also have one clear main purpose. Other measures, especially the 'green interventions', often have multiple microclimate functions, as you can see in the overview on the back flap.

The solutions are also categorized according to their spatial embedding: interventions directly connected to buildings, in parks and gardens, on squares, in streets or parking areas. Small icons represent these spatial types and can be found both in the catalogue and in the overview on the book flap. This overview is also organized according to these spatial types. For most types of interventions, the fact-sheet catalogue includes information on their effectiveness and extra advantages and/or disadvantages. When the pros clearly outweigh the cons, I conclude that you can consider these as no regret interventions. The catalogue also offers information about the construction and maintenance of several measures, as well as a relative indication of their costs. When it comes to wind measures, we can't speak of general pros and cons. Wind can form both a problem and a potential, so the measures for wind adaptation strongly depend on the conditions at a specific location or of a project. Also, wind patterns have no 'scale', so it is difficult to make statements about, for example, the costs of an intervention, since that depends on the scale of that particular intervention. The psychological aspects are also more generally applicable, so their description is different as well.

Before the detailed list of all measures described in the fact-sheet catalogue, this chapter offers a short, general discussion of the different aspects of influencing temperature and wind experience, rain protection and the psychological aspects. This includes a summary of the way the different types of solutions work (in close relation to chapter 2), and which aspects you should keep in mind when implementing these types of interventions.

6.1 Designing for Physical Temperature Experience

Here, I would like to emphasize again the importance of sun/ shadow, thermal radiation of materials and the air temperature on people's temperature experience. You can adapt all these aspects with small-scale solutions. Some of these solutions are very effective, and some of them less so. On a small-scale level, you can influence sun and shadow patterns very effectively. The interventions to temper the air temperature through evaporation on a small-scale level often have only a limited effect. To realize a greater effect, you have to implement these interventions to lower the air temperature on the scale of at least an entire district, and ideally combine them with shadow functions. Trees offer an ideal combination by casting shadow and evapotranspiration.

One theme is left out of this chapter: the reduction of anthropogenic heat. It is impossible for an urban designer to stop a city's warming through the exhaust fumes and motor heat of car traffic on a small scale. Solutions for this problem are to be found more in the design of the vehicles themselves. In the future, most cars will be electric, so we can expect this source of heat to disappear. We can, however, stop the extra warming caused by badly insulated buildings and air conditioners with careful adjustments to the buildings or by building new passive houses, ultra-low energy buildings. These building solutions have been elaborately discussed in the literature on sustainable architecture, so they are not included here.

One of the most influential factors of the microclimate that affect the way people experience temperature is the presence of shortwave solar radiation – so if someone is in the sun or in the shade. This radiation is much lower in the shadow than it is in direct sunlight. Therefore, the configuration of buildings in relation to the sun or shadow is important, as is the strategic placement of elements that provide shade, such as planting and street and garden furniture. From an urban climate point of view, green elements are always preferred, as their evapotranspiration lowers the air temperature. Many cases demand a location-specific design for sun and shadow, keeping in mind all continuously changing shadow patterns. That is why some design recommendations in the catalogue are more of a method for 'research by design'. This means you first map the existing conditions using shadow simulations (in SketchUp, AutoCad or similar programs), and then testing the different alternatives in order to find the optimal place for elements. You can find the solutions to influence sun and shadow on pages 113-148.

Influencing sun and shade

Influencing reflection

The reflection of shortwave radiation, or albedo, has a big impact on the storage of heat in a certain material. Especially smooth and light materials have a higher albedo. Using these types of materials can increase the albedo of large parts of the city. There are some issues you should consider when using materials with a higher albedo. When many reflecting materials are used in streets to keep walls (and thus indoor spaces) cool, eventually more shortwave radiation will be reflected into the street space. This shortwave radiation then hits objects again, but also people in the street. It is therefore best to only increase reflection in street spaces when there are no other options. In larger spaces such as squares raising the albedo can sometimes be useful. The big sky view factor allows the radiation to escape into the space above the city. You will find the chart with the albedo of different materials in illustration 10 on page 34 and the overview of reflection-influencing interventions on pages 149-154.

Influencing emissivity and heat conductivity

The radiation emission characteristics of materials are also crucial for the urban energy balance. In principle, all materials store heat. They do so to different extents and emit it at different speeds. Depending on the desired effect – whether you want to create cooler or warmer places – you can use different materials. When indoor or outdoor areas have to stay cool in summer because many people use these areas, it is advisable to use building materials that store less heat. When you want to create places that offer extra warmth in cooler seasons, you can use other suitable materials to influence this. You will find the chart with the emissivity and thermal conduction of different materials in illustration 10 on page 34 and the overview of interventions on pages 155-159.

Influencing evaporation

Evaporation is a crucial factor in the tempering of the air temperature (also see section 2.1.2). Evaporation occurs at the surfaces of water bodies and from water in the soil, but especially through the evapotranspiration from the stomata of plants. You can speed up the evaporation of water by spraying it as finely as possible. The enlarged surface of the fine drops strongly enhances evaporation. Still or slow-moving water bodies thus evaporate less water, and they also retain warmth. They can sometimes even be warmer than their surroundings. Therefore it is very important to move the water or preferably spray it for an effective cooling of the environment, or to have water evaporate through plants' evapotranspiration. You will find the solutions for influencing evaporation on pages 161-174.

6.2 Designing for Physical Wind Experience

Wind flows in urban areas can be both a problem and a potential. At some locations and especially in the cooler seasons, people have to be protected from the wind. At other locations and especially during heat waves, sufficient ventilation is in order. Therefore, you should first make a careful analysis of the location, use and period you will be designing for. Analysis and design overlap here, so make sure you have read sections 2.2.3 and 5.1.2.

Relating wind pattern analysis and design

It has to be clear from the start which human activities (such as walking or cycling) the design is for, and at which times the locations are in use. For example: is a seating area only meant for the summer or for other seasons as well? Does an urban area need ventilation on warm nights or doesn't it, since nobody stays there at night? The design should address these exact situations. But the other climate situations should not be overlooked in the analysis and the design, to prevent nuisances at other times of the year. This requires a study of the location's wind data. You can often download the data from the nearest weather station from the websites of meteorological institutes. Sometimes you get wind roses and sometimes you get the numerical data for further analysis in a spreadsheet.

The main questions in the wind-climate situation concern the problems and potentials. For possible problems, we should know: which wind from which direction is the strongest (with wind speeds of over 5 metre per second)? Does this wind occur often? This wind is usually not pleasant and has to be slowed down. For the potentials of wind to ventilate hot areas, the questions are different: which wind directions and speeds prevail on the warmest days? Is this wind strong enough (at least 2 metres per second) to offer ventilation? If not, what are the potentials for ventilation with local breezes (coastal, valley or local wind)?

What is also special about designing with wind is that wind patterns are primarily determined by the combination of volumes and open spaces. It is important to keep in mind that wind does not actually 'know' if a certain volume is a building, an earthen wall or very dense planting. It is just an obstacle for the air to flow around. Thinking in terms of 'volumes' and 'open spaces' is therefore essential. These proportions usually have no scale, because the flow patterns are the same on all scales. Because of this 'sliding scale', you will find some solutions in this chapter that basically match those on the city scale. In urban design, it is generally better to shape the urban tissue with the wind patterns in mind from the start. Retrofitting for these problems on the small scale is less efficient. Nonetheless, you will find extensive

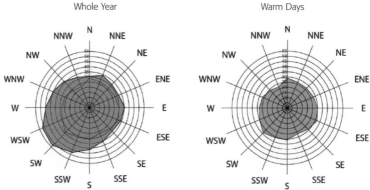

Whole Year   Warm Days

79 *Example of spreadsheet wind roses for the Dutch weather station Herwijnen (wind speeds in 0.1 metre per second)*

descriptions of these solutions in this chapter, because our cities are hardly ever designed from scratch (anymore), and a large part of the urban tissue is already there, so we'll have to work with local adjustments.

Slowing or avoiding wind

As we know from section 2.2, all objects (landscape and building volumes) and their mutual configurations create typical wind flow patterns. Some of those lead to such big wind problems that these have to be addressed in situ, or that it is better to avoid these locations for certain uses. The typical places for these problems to arise are for example the sides of larger buildings, because of the corner streams; the foot of high-rise buildings; and places where urban spaces narrow. Of course, the precise location of these places always depends on the wind. You will find the solutions for slowing the wind on pages 175-189.

Ventilation

Some outdoor places have to be ventilated well on hot days, especially in densely built-up residential areas. The little wind there is on hot days usually does not have a clear direction, and therefore we should primarily make use of local breezes. These are firstly the cooling valley winds we find in cities with larger differences in elevation in their relief. Another type of ventilation is the local urban wind between warmed-up and cooler areas in the city or at the city edges. When the courses of the cool airflows are clear, you can address those in your design. Ventilation is mainly about channelling wind and guiding it to the desired locations. You will find the solutions for channelling wind and ventilation on pages 190-193.

6.3 Designing for Protection Against Precipitation

Even though the precipitation we are exposed to doesn't play a very big role in our normal experience of the microclimate, it can really be a nuisance to us from time to time. Hence, it is very important to create protection against precipitation, especially rain. Precipitation protection is usually only planned for bus and tram shelters or train station roofs. But people should also be better protected from rain at other places, such as shopping streets or on large squares along important pedestrian routes. This is especially important for older people, who need more time to cross a square for instance and who might have to rest for a little. Considering most of our societies' ageing populations, we have to take this into account more often. Sidewalk cafes and smoking areas and such can often also be provided with better rain protection. Generally speaking, many solutions for creating shade can offer protection against precipitation as well. Many of these solutions do have a downside however: it is relatively dark underneath and this might not be nice on rainy days. You will therefore find some alternatives on page 195-197.

6.4   Designing for Multiple Microclimate Factors

In this book, we have seen a couple of times that certain interventions influence the microclimate in more than one way. Particularly 'green' solutions offer many advantages. But there are many more possible multifunctional combinations! You will find a number of these types of combinations in the last part of the catalogue. This entails inspirational examples that have not been realized yet, designed by me and partially together with my students. All examples are smaller installations or elements that can be placed in gardens and parks as well as in squares. They reflect how you can playfully address the microclimate in your designs. You will find these examples of multifunctional objects for influencing the microclimate on pages 199-208.

6.5   Designing for Psychological Aspects of Microclimate Experience

As we know, how people experience the microclimate does not only depend on purely physical factors such as radiation temperature, air temperature, wind and clothing. It also depends on the surroundings and what we can call 'ambiance'. As discussed in chapter 2, spaces can have a 'warm' or 'cold' ambiance with characteristics that have no thermal effect, and this ambiance influences the microclimate experience too. You can influence these factors significantly with spatial interventions, thus manipulating the way people will experience the space. Interventions to influence the ambiance can come in so many different shapes and forms, and can be applied in so many different places that there is no point in discussing their construction, maintenance and costs. These interventions are sketched on pages 209-212.

6.6   Implementation of Measures on the Micro-Scale Level

You will find more elaborate descriptions of the abovementioned smaller-scale solutions in the fact-sheet catalogue. All these measures can be implemented in very different ways, by different actors and in different amounts of time.
The owners of houses, office buildings and companies, for example, can make the surroundings of their buildings 'greener' or take wind-protection measures. The owners of brownfield areas have an opportunity to improve the urban climate relatively quickly, without many procedures, by implementing temporary green measures or by allowing urban agriculture on their land. Small changes on buildings, like a different use of colour or building materials, and changing facades, can usually be implemented relatively easily by owners. Governments could consider supporting these 'green' interventions on private properties that improve the entire urban climate with special subsidies. Some municipalities already grant such subsidies for green roofs. These subsidies could be a good incentive for other climate adaptations, such as green facades, 'de-surfacing' gardens or planting more trees in them.

When existing public spaces have to be adapted for the microclimate, municipalities can adopt this in their plans for redevelopment, for instance for urban renewal, shopping districts, inner cities and parks. Within the framework of such plans, measures can then be implemented relatively fast. A more 'gradual' adaptation can be realized by including measures in regulations concerning the continuous adjustment of a city's public spaces. In some cities, for example, city services have 'guidelines' for public space design, and the climate adaptation measures can be incorporated in these. Many possibilities for adaptation regarding street profiles, such as materialization, planting and choice of trees and furniture in streets, can be fixed in these guidelines. It is also possible to include microclimate interventions such as placing trees in streets and on squares, green facades and such in design ordinances that address the visual quality of districts, such as the German 'Gestaltungssatzung' and the Dutch 'Beeldkwaliteitsplan'.

Other somewhat bigger interventions, such as regulations for microclimate-driven building and street configurations are generally the responsibility of municipalities. This usually concerns plans for new districts. For extensive adjustments of existing areas, municipalities have to make changes in their zoning plans. These interventions therefore take the longest to implement. The municipality should check if the zoning plan's regulations are indeed followed. That implementation through zoning plans does generally work, is demonstrated by examples from the German city of Stuttgart, where measures to keep cold airflow streams clear, for example, have been taken up in the zoning plans.

Generally speaking, many changes to the urban climate can be realized with small measures that are usually easy to implement, provided these are consequently applied in many places. For example: if residents of a neighbourhood with many 'surfaced' gardens remove the tiles from their gardens and replace these with trees, such a neighbourhood can evolve from climatope-type 'city' to 'garden city', which has a much milder microclimate. So the sum of many small interventions can have great cumulative effects!

6.7 Catalogue of Measures to Influence the Microclimate

Influencing
Sun and Shade

Covered Spaces Beneath Buildings

1. **General information** If for some reason you want a location to be in the shade for a prolonged period of time, one possibility is to offer shade directly beneath a building. In principle, a building can be 'lifted', to create a columned hall underneath, a covered continuation of the outdoor space. Market halls used to be created in this way beneath town halls. In the days when there were no refrigerators and such, passive cooling through shadow was the best way to keep perishable goods fresh.

2. **Effectiveness** These spaces are cool, shaded and ventilated throughout the year.

3. **Extra advantages** The advantage of these spaces is that they offer shading and protection from the weather without extra costs for cooling.

4. **Disadvantages** It can be too dark and draughty in winter. The natural cooling in these spaces is not as effective as that in a modern covered space, acclimatized with air conditioning. The allocation of private and public ground property can be a problem. Many building owners have objections when parts of their building are publicly accessible.

5. **Construction** The construction of these open, covered spaces is an integral part of the construction of the building.

6. **Maintenance** The maintenance is part of the normal maintenance of the building.

7. **Costs** € € € (depending on the size of the building)

8. No regret: No

80 *The former market hall in Stresa, Italy, beneath the old town hall*

Arcades

1. **General information** When people want to be in the direct surroundings of a building or when they want to walk alongside the building while being protected – when they are shopping, for instance – arcades are a traditional option for offering shade.

2. **Effectiveness** If arcades are well adjusted to the positions of the sun, they allow the sun to come in during the winter, when it has low angles, whilst protecting people from the bright sun in the summer (high angles). Shadow simulations are needed to establish the best height and width of the arcade.

3. **Extra advantages** Arcades are a robust solution to offer shelter from the sun and other weather circumstances. The arcade spaces can have several functions, and enrich a city's diversity in microclimates.

4. **Disadvantages** The ground ownership conditions of arcade space can sometimes be a problem. To solve this, you need solid arrangements of whether the space is in public ownership at street level, and the building above it in private ownership; or whether it is better to have the street level area be privately owned as well, with the public having right of way.

5. **Construction** Arcades usually have to be part of the construction plans from the start. It is sometimes possible to build arcades later, but then it is often more difficult to fit the arcade into the architecture and the costs are much higher.

6. **Maintenance** The maintenance is part of the normal maintenance of the building.

7. **Costs** € € € (depending on the size and length of the arcade)

8. **No regret:** yes

81 *A classic arcade at the Plaza Mayor in Madrid, Spain*

Loggias

1. **General information** To offer a shaded, open place as part of a building that is well protected from the influences of the weather, loggias can be used. The height and depth of loggias should be well adjusted to the positions of the sun.
2. **Effectiveness** Providing the loggias have a good depth and are not facing north, they can offer protection from the bright, high-summer sun, whilst allowing the low evening and winter sun to come in. The same goes for the spaces of the building behind the loggias, where people live or work.
3. **Extra advantages** Besides effective sun protection, loggias also offer good protection from the rain and wind. Plus, they offer more privacy than balconies.
4. **Disadvantages** None
5. **Construction** Loggias have to be part of the building plans from the start.
6. **Maintenance** The maintenance is part of the normal maintenance of the building.
7. **Costs** € €
8. **No regret:** yes
8 **No regret:** ja

82 *A loggia in the University Quarter of Dortmund, Germany*

Canopies and Louvres

1. **General information** When people want to sit on a balcony or terrace, canopies and louvres are an option for offering shadow. Patio covers are closed roofs and louvres consist of a frame with small horizontal strips of wood.
2. **Effectiveness** Both options provide good shading.
3. **Extra advantages** Besides sun protection, these solutions also provide some protection from the rain. Canopies and louvres allow for smart combinations, for example placing solar panels or solar installations on top of the coverings.
4. **Disadvantages** Canopies and louvres are fixed and the spaces beneath them might not get enough sun at certain times. This depends on the precise placement of the elements.
5. **Construction** Canopies and louvres can be an integral part of the construction of a building, or they can be placed afterwards.
6. **Maintenance** These elements are relatively robust and low-maintenance because they are fixed to the building.
7. **Costs** € €
8. **No regret:** no

83 *A louvre at a pavilion in Barcelona, Spain*

Flexible Awnings

1. **General information** If people wish to sit on a terrace right next to a building, there are several options for fixing shading objects to the building. You can open or close these to your liking. Think of classic parasols and awnings, but also less common elements such as canopies and horizontal sunscreens. You can also think of folding or sliding panel-type constructions.

2. **Effectiveness** Because of their flexibility, people can use these solutions for all kinds of weather circumstances, so they are very effective.

3. **Extra advantages** The flexibility means that there are many more options than with fixed solutions. If the material is strong and impermeable, these solutions can also provide rain protection.

4. **Disadvantages** Because of their lightweight construction, flexible systems are usually more vulnerable than fixed solutions, and the life span of textile awnings is relatively short.

5. **Construction** Flexible awnings can be an integral part of the construction of a building, or they can be placed afterwards.

6. **Maintenance** The systems need regular maintenance (for instance cleaning and oiling).

7. **Costs** € €

8. **No regret:** Yes

84 *Sliding panels in front of balconies, Dortmund, Germany*

Planted Pergolas

1. **General information** Attached to buildings, but also as freestanding objects, pergolas are a good option for shading. Pergolas are usually lightweight constructions with light beams or wires supporting climbing plants. These climbing plants can be deciduous (e.g. kiwi, vines, aristolochia, wisteria, climbing hydrangea and many others) or evergreen (e.g. ivy).

2. **Effectiveness** Depending on the density of the foliage, the shadow effect can be lighter or deeper. But the effect on solar radiation can easily come to a 50 per cent reduction. Obviously, a pergola can also reduce the solar radiation on adjacent walls.

3. **Extra advantages** If deciduous plants are chosen and a pergola construction that is not too heavy, the pergola will allow sun penetration in winter. The plants offer extra cooling through evapotranspiration.

4. **Disadvantages** Pergolas are more permeable to rain than closed roofs are.

5. **Construction** Pergolas can be constructed relatively easily – also by practiced laymen. Keep in mind that the foundation has to be able to support the construction and the extra weight of the plants.

6. **Maintenance** Pergolas require regular maintenance (painting, touching up on the woodworks) and some plants require regular pruning.

7. **Costs** € €

8. **No regret:** Yes

85 *A pergola attached to an office building in Essen, Germany*

Espalier Trees at a Distance from a Building

1. **General information** To shade windows of houses in a natural way and thus prevent overheating of living spaces, you can use espalier trees. These trees are placed several metres from the buildings and are usually no taller than 5 metres. They are usually pruned in a candelabra-like manner. The tree types (usually lime trees) are fast growing and yearly pruning takes place in autumn. Because of this, they hardly have any branches in winter, but when spring comes, the trees quickly grow branches and leaves for summer shading. The desired height of these branches depends on the height of the windows and the position of the sun. Espalier trees are a very classic example of influencing the microclimate, and you can sometimes find them on old farms in Central Europe.

2. **Effectiveness** The espalier trees are reasonably effective, providing they are planted in the right spot and are maintained well, but they are less effective than flexible awnings are.

3. **Extra advantages** The trees' evapotranspiration helps temper the air temperature. In some places, these trees can also be used to demarcate owners' premises.

4. **Disadvantages** Espaliers create less shadow in outdoor spaces and are therefore less suitable for providing shade outdoors.

5. **Construction** Young espalier trees are usually provided with a supporting construction for the branches to be trained along. If they are old enough for the branch-structure to have the desired shape, this support is no longer needed.

6. **Maintenance** The special shape of espalier trees and the need to allow for winter sun also mean they have to be meticulously and expertly pruned every year.

7. **Costs** € €

8. **No regret:** Yes

86 Espalier lime trees in front of an old house in Rotterdam, the Netherlands

Green Facades

1. General information You can use very different types of facade planting to shade buildings so as to reduce the heating of walls and thus the indoor spaces. Classic green facades consist of climbers planted in the earth, but there are two different types of climbing plants. Firstly, there are plants that fix themselves to the walls with small 'suckers' or root hairs (e.g. ivy, climbing hydrangea or wild vines), and secondly there are plants that climb by curling around threads and lattices and such (most other climbing plants).

Another classic type of green facade is fruit trees pruned in shape and guided along the walls with threads. The trees profit extra from the longwave radiation of the building, so their fruits ripen more quickly.

New systems have been developed over the past few decades, in which plant containers are part of the facade. Different types of plants (including non-climbers) that can

87 Four types of green facades: self-climbing plants, supported climbers, plant containers in facades and vertical gardens

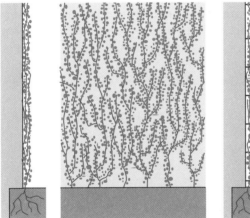

Self-climbing plants in deep soil

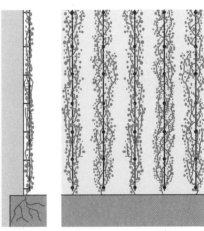

Climbers supported through wires or lattices

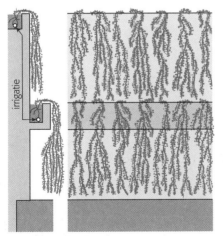

irrigatie

Built- in or attached planters

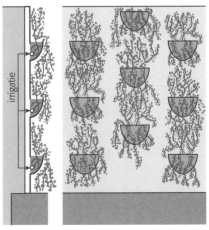

irrigatie

Panels or plastic 'curtains' with small plant containers

grow with limited space for their roots are used for these planters.

The latest development is 'vertical gardens', covering large parts of walls like tapestries. These are in fact separate plants, growing from many small compartments. These compartments consist of small pots or bags fixed to a large grid or cloth, which is directly attached to the wall.

2. **Effectiveness** The shadow-effect of planted facades is very strong. Planted facades can lead to a decrease in temperature of up to a maximum of 30 °C of the wall itself and up to a maximum of 3 °C in room temperature, thus using up to 40 per cent less energy for cooling.

3. **Extra advantages** The evapotranspiration of the plants in green facades helps temper the air temperature, but much less effectively than trees do. The buildings behind the green facades are simultaneously protected against influences from the weather. Another positive effect is the layer of air between the planted facade and the walls of the building. This layer offers insulation in winter and can reduce heat loss by approximately 6 per cent. This effect is of course stronger with ever-green plants. Green facades are often also a special addition to the architecture.

4. **Disadvantages** The availability of water for the plants can be a bottleneck. Especially plant systems that use plant containers need irrigation and this can be a big problem for large 'green tapestries'. Some people do not like it when birds and insects live in the facade-plants. Self-climbing plants can sometimes damage the stuccowork or wall when they have to be removed.

88 *Green facade in Antwerp, Belgium*

89 Vertical garden of Patrick Blanc, Caixa Forum, Madrid, Spain

5. **Construction** There are several ways to make a green facade. Self-climbing plants only need to be planted. Systems for supported climbing plants have to be well planned and require stable constructions. Plant container systems and 'green tapestries' are preferably an integral part of the building's design. Their construction is often complicated and requires the work of professionals.

6. **Maintenance** The plant systems using planters always require irrigation systems. These have to be checked and maintained on a regular basis. Especially with 'green tapestries', each small 'planting bag' in fact has to have its own irrigation scheme. This is often problematic and many plants die and have to be replaced. Systems with supported climbing plants have to be checked up upon once in a while.

7. **Costs** Self-climbing plants in deep soil €; Climbers in planters, supported climbers and trained fruit trees € €; green tapestries € € €.

8. **No regret:** Yes

Planted Screen Elements

1. **General information** For light shadowing to keep a building's walls from heating up too much, you can use several types of planted screen elements. These elements are placed at least 50 centimetres from the facade and can come in the shape of panels or pillars. How much shadow these elements will offer also depends on the supporting construction. Lightweight wire constructions, primarily functioning as support for climbers will not cast deep shadows themselves. Solid constructions such as plant containers will offer more shade even without the plants.

2. **Effectiveness** Planted screen elements are less effective when it comes to shading than direct greening of the walls would be. These elements do not have the advantage of an insulating layer of air and also do not provide as much protection against the weather.

3. **Extra advantages** The evapotranspiration of the plants helps temper the air temperature, but less effectively than trees do. Since the green elements are not directly attached to the walls, the walls are more easily accessible, for example for maintenance.

4. **Disadvantages** The availability of water for the plants can be a bottleneck when the weather is hot. Especially plant systems using planters need irrigation and proper fertilization.

5. **Construction** These systems always have to be well planned, think of such aspects as the weight of the plant containers and the supporting construction. Professionals have to be brought in for the construction.

6. **Maintenance** When climbers root in the earth, you normally do not need an extra irrigation system and only have to take care of the upkeep of the supporting construction. Systems using plant containers always require irrigation and fertilization.

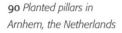

90 *Planted pillars in Arnhem, the Netherlands*

You have to carefully regulate, maintain and monitor these systems.

7. **Costs** Deep soil climbing plant systems € €, Climbers in planters € € €.

8. **No regret:** Yes

Built Elements Demarcating Plots

1. **General information** Elements demarcating plots are a category of potentially shading elements that is often overlooked. These demarcations are often stone walls, wooden fences or they are made of other building materials, and these can provide shading for the outdoor spaces of houses.

2. **Effectiveness** The surface areas shaded by the demarcation elements are obviously smaller than those shaded by vertical sun protection, but depending on the size of the demarcations, the shaded areas can be quite large.

3. **Extra advantages** Demarcation elements provide shading and wind protection, but their main function is to protect people's property and privacy. Drywalls and wattle fences can also be home to small animals such as lizards.

4. **Disadvantages** Demarcation elements can cast long shadows in winter. Some demarcations that retain much heat (e.g. stone constructions) can emit heat in the evening, which may be an undesired side effect.

5. **Construction** The construction of demarcations can be simple (such as the wooden fences you can buy at DIY stores), but can also require real workmanship, for instance for beautifully crafted masonry.

6. **Maintenance** The maintenance depends on the type of demarcation. Walls usually require very little maintenance, whereas wooden fences have to be painted regularly.

7. **Costs** Depending on the type € to € €

8. **No regret:** No

91 *A slate drywall as demarcation*

Green Demarcation Elements

1. **General information** Green demarcation elements, such as fences planted with climbers or hedges can also provide considerable shading.
2. **Effectivenes** The surface areas shaded by the green demarcation elements are obviously smaller than those shaded by vertical sun protection, but depending on the size of the elements, the shaded areas can be quite large.
3. **Extra advantages** Demarcation elements offer shading and wind protection, but their main function is to protect people's property and privacy. Green demarcation elements also lower the air temperature through evapotranspiration. In winter, deciduous green demarcations do not cast much shadow, which can be advantageous for the sun exposure of a house.
4. **Disadvantages** Dense, evergreen demarcation elements can cast too much shadow in winter.
5. **Construction** Hedges and shrubs as green demarcation elements are relatively easy to implement. Professional work is preferred when the plants grow on grids or other construction types.
6. **Maintenance** Green demarcation elements have to be pruned on an occasional to regular basis.
7. **Costs** €
8. **No regret:** Yes

92 *Planted fences, Jardins d'Eole, Paris, France*

Park Trees and Shrubs

1. **General information** To create shading, planting more trees and shrubs is the most obvious solution. They can also significantly reduce the solar radiation on buildings. Depending on the desired shadow effect, the choice is between deciduous or evergreen trees. In more densely built surroundings, where buildings cast long shadows in winter, deciduous trees are usually preferable, to prevent too many places from being shaded. Tree types also differ considerably in the size and density of their foliage. This obviously influences the depth of the shadow (see list illustration 94). Considering the effect of future circumstances (due to climate change) on the types of trees that can grow in our latitudes, we have to make suitable choices of tree species. To this end, there are lists of trees and shrubs in temperate climate zones that are 'climate proof' and thus can stand more heat and drought (see list illustration 95).

2. **Effectiveness** The tree's shadow intercepts much of the incoming radiation. This leads to a reduction in solar radiation of up to 50 per cent on the surfaces beneath. The shadow, however, is not as dense as that of objects that are impenetrable to solar radiation (such as walls) and strongly depends on the chosen species (see list illustration 94).

3. **Extra advantages** Trees and shrubs also have a significant effect when it comes to tempering the air temperature through evapotranspiration. Besides the microclimatic effect, they have many other positive effects. They can filter air and noise; produce timber, fruit and nuts; increase biodiversity; and highlight the changing of the seasons. When buildings are surrounded by beautiful, big trees, this can even raise their real estate value.

4. **Disadvantages** Trees attract animals and insects, which might be an undesired side effect.

5. **Construction** Planting trees and shrubs is usually quite simple, provided that the soil conditions are suitable and there is sufficient room for the roots.

6. **Maintenance** Because of their growth and the leaves they grow, trees and shrubs do need maintenance.

7. **Costs** €

8. **No regret:** Yes

93 *Large park tree in Copenhagen, Denmark*

94 *List of shadow depths of trees*

Botanical name	Common English name	Transmissivity range (%) summer	winter	a) Foliation	b) Defoliation
Acer platanoides	Norway maple	5-14	60-75	E	M
Acer rubrum	Red Maple	8-22	63-82	M	E
Acer saccharinum	Silver maple	10-28	60-87	M	M
Acer saccharum	Sugar maple	16-27	60-80	M	E
Aesculus hippocastanum	Horse-chestnut	8-27	73	M	L
Amelanchier canadensis	Canadian serviceberry	20-25	57	L	M
Betula pendula	Silver birch	14-24	48-88	M	M-L
Carya ovata	Shagbark hickory	15-28	66		
Catalpa speciosa	Western catalpa	24-30	52-83	L	
Fagus sylvatica	European beech	7-15	83	L	L
Fraxinus pennsylvanica	Green Ash	10-29	70-71	M-L	M
Gleditsia tricanthos inermis	Honeylocust	25-50	50-85	M	E
Juglans nigra	Black walnut	9		L	E-M
Liriodendron tulipifera	Tulip tree	10	55-72	M-L	M
Picea pungens	Colorado spruce	13-28	69-78		
Pinus strobus	White pine	25-30	13-28		
Platanus acerifolia	London plane tree	11-17	25-30	L	M-L
Populus deltoides	Cottonwood	10-20	46-64	E	M
Populus tremuloides	Trembling aspen	20-33	68	E	M
Quercus alba	White oak	13-38			
Quercus rubra	Red oak	12-23	70-81	M	M
Tilia cordata	Littleleaf lime	7-22	46-70	L	E
Ulmus americana	American elm	13	63-89	M	M

a) E = Early   = before April 30 st
   M = Middle   = May 1st - 15th
   L = Late   = after May 15 st

b) E = Early   = before Nov 1 st
   M = Middle   = Nov 1st - 30st
   L = Late   = after Nov 30 st

Botanical name	Common English name	Frost hardiness
Acer campestre	Field maple	++
Acer negundo	Ash-leaved maple	++
Acer opalus	Italian Maple	+
Acer rubum	Red Maple	+
Acer x zoeschense	Maple "Zoeschen"	++
Ailanthus altissima	Tree of heaven	+
Alnus incana	Grey alder	++
Carya tomentosa	Mockernut hickory	+
Catalpa speciosa	Northern catalpa	+
Cedrus brevifolia	Cyprus cedar	+
Cedrus libani	Lebanon cedar	+
Celtis caucasia	Caucasian Hackberry	+
Celtis occidentalis	Common hackberry	+
Cladrastis sinensis	Yellowwood	++
Cupressus arizonica	Arizona cypress	+
Diospyros lotus	Date-plum	+
Fraxinus angustifolia	Narrow-leafed Ash	+
Fraxinus pallisiae	Pallis' Ash	++
Fraxinus quadrangulata	Blue ash	+
Ginkgo biloba	Gingko	+
Gleditsia japonica	Japanese Honey Locust	+
Gleditsia triacanthos	Honey locust	+
Juniperus communis	Common juniper	++
Juniperus scopulorum	Rocky Mountain Juniper	++
Juniperus virginiana	Pencil cedar	++
Maackia amurensis	Amur maackia	+
Ostrya carpinifolia	Hop Hornbeam	++
Ostrya virginiana	American hop hornbeam	+
Phellodendron sachalinense	Sachalin Cork-tree	++
Pinus bungeana	Lacebark pine	+
Pinus heldreichii	Bosnian pine	++
Pinus nigra	Black pine	++
Pinus ponderosa	Western yellow pine	+
Pinus rigida	Nothern pine	+
Pinus sylvestris	Scots pine	++
Platanus x hispania	London plane	+
Populus alba	White poplar	+
Prunus avium	Wild cherry	++
Quercus bicolor	Swamp white oak	++
Quercus cerris	Turkey oak	+
Quercus coccinea	Scarlet oak	+
Quercus frainetto	Hungarian oak	+
Quercus macranthera	Caucasian oak	+
Quercus macrocarpa	Bur oak	++
Quercus montana	Chestnut oak	+
Quercus muehlenbergii	Chinkapin oak	+
Quercus pubescens	Downy oak	+
Robinia pseudoacacia	Locust	++
Robinia viscosa	Clammy locust	++
Sophora japonica	Pagoda Tree	+

++ very good   + good

Sorbus aria	Whitebeam	++
Sorbus badensis	European mountainash	++
Sorbus domestica	Service tree	+
Sorbus latifolia	Service tree of Fontainebleau	+
Sorbus tominalis	Wild service tree	+
Sorbus x thuringiaca	Sorbus "Fastigiata"	++
Thuja orientalis	Eastern arbor-vitae	+
Tilia mandshurica	Mandshurian Linden	++
Tilia tomentosa	Silver lime	+
Ulmus pumila	Siberian elm	++

++ very good   + good

Botanical name	Common English name	Frost hardiness
Acer buergerianum	Trident maple	++
Acer platanoides	Norway maple	++
Aesculus x carnea	Red horse-chestnut	++
Alnus cordata	Italian Alder	+
Alnus x spaethii	Alder "Spaethii"	++
Betula pendula	Silver birch	++
Carpinus betulus	Common hornbeam	++
Carya ovata	Shagbark hickory	+
Castanea sativa	Sweet chestnut	+
Celtis bungeana	Bunge's hackberry	+
Corylus colurna	Turkish hazel	+
Cupressocyparis leylandii	Leyland cypress	+
Diospyros virginiana	American persimmon	+
Eucommia ulmoides	Gutta-percha tree	+
Fraxinus excelsior	European ash	+
Fraxinus pennsylvanica	Green ash	++
Gymnocladus dioica	Kentucky coffeetree	+
Malus tschonoskii	Chonosuki crab apple	++
Nyssa sylvatica	Tupelo	+
Phellodendron amurense	Amur cork tree	+
Picea omorika	Serbian spruce	++
Pinus peuce	Macedonian pine	+
Platanus occidentalis	American plane tree	+
Populus x berolinensis	Poplar "Berlin"	++
Populus tremula	Aspen	++
Pyrus communis	Common pear	+
Pyrus pyraster	European wild pear	+
Quercus imbricaria	Shingle oak	+
Quercus palustris	Pin oak	+
Quercus robur ssp. Sessiliflora	Pedunculate oak	+
Quercus rubra	Northern red oak	+
Sorbus intermedia	Swedish whitebeam	++
Tilia cordata	Littleleaf lime	++
Tilia x euchlora	Caucasian lime	++
Ulmus parvifolia	Chinese elm	+
Zelkova serrata	Japanese zelkova	+

++ very good   + good

Perennial Plants with Very Large Leaves

1. **General information** As a green alternative for woody vegetation, you can also use perennial plants with large leaves for shading. Think of Gunnera macrophylla, tree ferns and such.
2. **Effectiveness** The effectiveness is comparable to that of trees and shrubs, so you can expect a radiation reduction of up to 50 per cent under the leaves.
3. **Extra advantages** Such perennial trees have one large advantage: they retreat in winter. So in this period, they do not cast any shadow. Moreover, they often have a very special appearance and great aesthetic value.
4. **Disadvantages** None
5. **Construction** Planting perennials is easy when the soil and growth circumstances are suitable.
6. **Maintenance** Such perennial plants sometimes require special care.
7. **Costs** €
8. **No regret:** Yes

96 *A Gunnera macrophylla can be used for shading, Dublin, Ireland*

Colonnades and Pavilions

1. **General information** If, for certain reasons, plant elements are not wanted, you can also choose built objects. The reasons for this less optimal solution may concern maintenance, aesthetics or be of a functional nature. These small buildings can be meant for people to relax in (pavilions) or move through (colonnades) while being shaded. You can provide these buildings with fixed or flexible shading elements.

2. **Effectiveness** If the buildings do not let any sun in at all, the shadow effect is much stronger than it is with plants, and there is almost no incoming shortwave radiation.

3. **Extra advantages** The built elements can often add something special to a space. It is also possible to install photovoltaic systems or solar installations on the roofs.

4. **Disadvantages** These built elements absorb extra heat and emit longwave radiation, so they can, to a small degree, add to a higher air temperature.

5. **Construction** Depending on the desired form, the construction can be simple or be really specialist work.

6. **Maintenance** Wooden constructions require more maintenance than stone or metal constructions.

7. **Costs** € €

8. **No regret:** No

97 Colonnade in Parc de la Villette, Paris, France

Green Pavilions and Arbours

1. **General information** A good compromise neutralizing the disadvantages of built shadow elements (regarding heat absorption and radiation) are lightweight architectural objects with plants growing on them. These can be made of lightweight masonry, with slats, wires and such, along which plants can climb.

2. **Effectiveness** Similar to pergolas, the shadow effect can be lighter or deeper, depending on the density of growth. The deflected radiation is often a little over 50 per cent, because the construction's shadow and that of the vegetation add up.

3. **Extra advantages** The positive aspects of a small building as a shadow element (e.g. a special shape) are combined with the advantages of vegetation here: the plants provide cooling and block solar radiation, which would otherwise be absorbed by the building and emitted as heat.

4. **Disadvantages** None

5. **Construction** The construction of green pavilions and arbours can be complicated and you have to calculate for the weight of the plants.

6. **Maintenance** The construction requires upkeep, and the plants can make that difficult. The plants themselves need regular care as well.

7. **Costs** € €

8. **No regret:** Yes

98 *Green canopy, Lincoln Park, Miami, USA*

Shadow Roofs

1. **General information** Since urban squares generally require space for circulation and to provide an open visual field on eye level, shadow roofs resting on only a few pillars are useful here. These objects can be made with flexible textile elements or fixed roof-like constructions.

2. **Effectiveness** If the elements block the sun entirely, the shadow effect is good, but because these elements are often on pillars and the roof isn't very large, more sun can come in from the sides.

3. **Extra advantages** The built elements can be a special addition to a space. You can also install photovoltaic systems on or in the roofs.

4. **Disadvantages** These built elements absorb extra heat and emit longwave radiation, so they can, to a small degree, add to a higher air temperature. When these objects have flexible elements, these may be vulnerable to vandalism.

5. **Construction** Depending on the desired construction, making these objects can be relatively simple or be specialist work.

6. **Maintenance** Wooden constructions need more maintenance than metal constructions. It is not always easy to maintain constructions with flexible elements, because of the more vulnerable materials and moving parts. Fixed objects have these problems to a lesser degree.

7. **Costs** € €

8. **No regret:** No

99 *A shadow roof on a square in Barcelona, Spain*

Trees on Squares

1. **General information** Because the surrounding buildings often visually dominate urban squares, shadow trees can be used as a contrast. My experiential research in North-Western Europe has shown that people prefer to have more green elements on squares, especially trees. The possibilities for using trees are more limited on squares than in parks, though. Squares need to be surveyed and have to provide room for markets, events and such. Trees with crown bottoms that are relatively high above the ground are therefore preferable, and you shouldn't use much or any undergrowth. You also often have to take underground constructions such as car parks into account.

2. **Effectiveness** The tree's shadow intercepts much of the incoming radiation. This leads to a reduction in solar radiation of up to 50 per cent on the surfaces beneath. Trees also shade the paved surfaces of the squares, and as a result these absorb less energy and thus emit less heat.

3. **Extra advantages** Trees do not only offer shade; their evapotranspiration also tempers the air temperature. In winter, many trees lose their foliage, and thus their shadow effect is reduced, allowing for extra sun penetration. Moreover, trees have an important aesthetical function: they create an umbrageous ambiance, and this often attracts people. A single tree on a square can sometimes become a place for people to gather round.

4. **Disadvantages** Like all elements, trees can be obstacles, for instance on market days or when there is an event. A well-

100 *A typical 'tree square': the Lange Voorhout in The Hague, the Netherlands*

planned layout of the trees can prevent this, however, and there are ample examples where vegetation is not an obstacle, for instance at the big fair at the Lange Voorhout in The Hague or the Christmas market at the Neumarkt in Cologne. The available rooting space is always an issue with trees on squares, as is the availability of water and good aeration of the soil. Trees are often planted in smaller planting sites or in some cases even in containers with very limited rooting space, for instance when there is a car park beneath the square. Under these conditions, trees can only survive if they are virtually immune to stress. It is therefore crucial that you put in a lot of consideration before you decide what tree species to use.

5. **Construction** Specialists have to be the ones to plant trees on squares, because they often have to prepare specific planting sites with systems for aeration and irrigation.

6. **Maintenance** City trees need more care than trees in the landscape, because there are more stress factors in the city, such as heat, drought and road salt. Cleaning up the leaves and pruning are also a lot of work.

7. **Costs** € €

8. **No regret:** Yes

Built Shadow Elements in Streets

1. **General information** Above the sidewalks, all kinds of shadow elements can be fixed directly onto the buildings, as discussed before in the 'Around Buildings' section (see inner back flap). When there is sufficient space in boulevard-type street profiles, other small architectural structures such as freestanding roofs and pergolas can be used for shading. You can find descriptions of these elements in the 'In Gardens and Parks' and 'On Squares' sections (see inner back flap). A special type of elements is the 'shadow curtain': a flexible shadow element that can be spanned over a street.

2. **Effectiveness** If the elements block the sun entirely, the shadow effect directly under the curtains is good and there will be relatively little incoming shortwave radiation. Because these elements are often higher up in the street profile, to allow for traffic, more sun can come in from the sides.

3. **Extra advantages** The built elements can be a special aesthetic addition to a space. You can also install photovoltaic systems or sun boilers on the roofs of fixed structures.

4. **Disadvantages** Built elements can absorb extra heat and emit longwave radiation, so they can, to a small degree, add to a higher air temperature. This is not a problem with textile elements. Flexible systems are generally more vulnerable, also to vandalism, and have a shorter lifespan.

5. **Construction** Depending on the desired construction, making these objects can be relatively simple or be specialist work.

6. **Maintenance** Wooden constructions require more maintenance than stonework or metal constructions do. The moving parts of flexible systems need special attention.

7. **Costs** € €

8. **No regret:** Fixed constructions – No; Flexible constructions – Yes

101 *Shadow curtain over a street, Santa Barbara, California, USA*

Street Trees

1. General information If you want a street to have continuous shading, trees are the most obvious and efficient solution. Rows of trees in streets have e great effect on the shading of the street itself and the surrounding facades. Because of the shadow, the usually black, asphalt street surface is not heated up as much, so eventually there will be less longwave radiation. You have to be very careful about what type of tree you choose, with regard to the deepness of the shadows (also see illustration 94). Deciduous trees are generally preferable, since they allow for more sun in the winter. The trees have to be planted in such a way that they fit into the street space and the daylighting of the adjacent buildings. In residential streets, trees should not block the sun coming into the houses in the winter. In streets where buildings have other functions, this is not always necessary.

Each street profile with its height-width ratios is different and the orientation of streets differs as well. The path of the sun is different for each place on earth too. All this results in very diverse shadow patterns. To address these unique situations with a design for tree rows, it is best to first make a simulation of the shadow patterns with the trees you want to plant. These shadow patterns can be visualized with 3D-software such as SketchUp and AutoCad. First, you need to know which areas in the street are most impacted by solar radiation. Shadow pattern simulations depicting the situation at 3 p.m. will suffice, because at that time the heat increase is at its top and the heat problems are biggest (see illustration 102). Next, you have to see where in the street profile most people stay or circulate, so you know which areas need good shading. You also have to check which buildings have windows that should not be shaded, and where you can't plant trees because of underground utility lines. Illustration 103 shows what this little study can look like for a shopping street and for a street with sidewalks. Finally, you can project trees of different heights and habitus on the street spaces, on the spots they can be planted in. The trees' shadows can then be simulated to test whether the areas with many people are

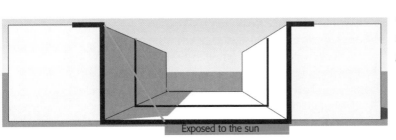

Exposed to the sun

102 Simulation of the shadow in a street at 3 p.m.

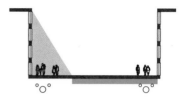

103 Analysing places, locating people, utility lines and windows

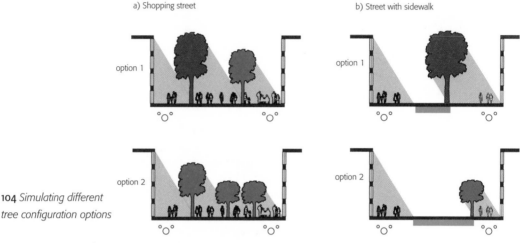

a) Shopping street

b) Street with sidewalk

option 1

option 1

option 2

option 2

104 Simulating different tree configuration options

shaded and the windows (if need be) are not (see illustration 104). There are usually many options here, leaving elbowroom for the designer.

2. **Effectiveness** Planted in the right spots, trees can intercept much incoming radiation and thus heating. They intercept up to 50 per cent of the solar radiation falling on the street surface and the facades.

3. **Extra advantages** Street trees are valuable for reasons of aesthetics, water management and ecology as well. They can also retain fine dust and air pollution.

4. **Disadvantages** Trees can sometimes obstruct ventilation. In streets with heavy traffic, this can slow the dispersion of air pollution. In these cases, the trees have to be planted with more space between them. This does, of course, diminish the shadow effect.

5. **Construction** Planting trees in streets is specialist work, because they often have to prepare specific planting sites with systems for aeration and irrigation. Other conditions sometimes have to be reckoned with, such as the location of underground utility lines and traffic lanes.

6. **Maintenance** Street trees need more care than trees in the countryside, because they are exposed to more stress factors

in the city, such as heat, drought and road salt. Cleaning up
the leaves and pruning are also a lot of work.

7. Costs € €

8. No regret: Yes

Carports

1. **General information** Carports or lightweight roof constructions above parking spaces can provide the necessary shading. Because cars have to be able to drive in and out, shadow elements should only take up limited surface space, for instance resting on just a few pillars.

2. **Effectiveness** If the elements block the sun entirely, the shadow effect is good, but because these elements are often on pillars and the roof isn't very large, more sun can come in from the sides.

3. **Extra advantages** The built elements can also block rain and other weather influences, and prevent the car from getting dirty because of pollen, leaves, bird droppings and such. It is also possible to place solar installations or photovoltaic elements on these roofs.

4. **Disadvantages** Built elements can absorb extra heat and emit longwave radiation, so they can, to a small degree, add to a higher air temperature.

5. **Construction** Building carports is usually relatively simple, but you do need professionals for large constructions.

6. **Maintenance** In general, carports are easy to maintain, but wooden constructions require more maintenance than metal constructions.

7. **Costs** € €

8. **No regret:** No

105 *Carports in Siedlung Schüngelberg, Gelsenkirchen, Germany*

Trees in Parking Lots

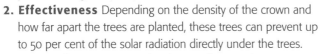

1. **General information** Trees can offer good shading for cars in outdoor car parks. It is important for efficient shading that trees have broad crowns and are not spaced out too much. Here too, the best way to decide where to plant the trees is to use shadow simulations during the design process, taking in the potential buildings too (see 'Street Trees', page 141-143). For parking lots it is generally better to use evergreen trees. This way, the trees offer shade in the summer and protections against precipitation in other seasons.

2. **Effectiveness** Depending on the density of the crown and how far apart the trees are planted, these trees can prevent up to 50 per cent of the solar radiation directly under the trees.

3. **Extra advantages** Besides the cars, large surfaces of asphalt are also shaded and thus protected from strong heating. Trees also offer extra cooling through evapotranspiration. They can have aesthetical and ecological value as well.

4. **Disadvantages** Trees parked under trees can have blossoms; leaves and fruit fall on them. Animals living in the tree can be nuisances because of their droppings (e.g. birds, plant lice).

5. **Construction** Gardeners should plant trees in parking lots, because they often have to prepare specific planting sites with systems for aeration and irrigation.

6. **Maintenance** Trees in parking lots require relatively much care, because they are exposed to more stress factors in the city, such as heat, drought and road salt. The trees sometimes need extra water in hot circumstances. Cleaning up the leaves and pruning are also a lot of work.

7. **Costs** €

8. **No regret:** Yes

106 *Parking lot with shadow trees in Duisburg, Germany*

Planted Shadow Elements

1. **General information** Pergola-type, green constructions can also provide shade in parking lots. Deciduous and evergreen plants can grow on these constructions. If you also want good rain protection in winter, evergreen vegetation is preferable.

2. **Effectiveness** Depending on the density of the foliage, the plants can shade a parking lot effectively.

3. **Extra advantages** Besides the cars, large surfaces of asphalt are also shaded and thus protected from strong heating. Plants also offer extra cooling through evapotranspiration. They can have aesthetical and ecological value as well.

4. **Disadvantages** Cars parked under pergolas can have blossoms; leaves and fruit fall on them. Animals living in the pergolas can be nuisances because of their droppings (e.g. birds, plant lice). Pergolas offer less rain protection than closed roofs do.

5. **Construction** Pergolas in car parks have to meet certain safety regulations and their foundations have to be strong enough to support the biomass. Therefore, it's best if professionals place the pergolas.

6. **Maintenance** Pergolas require regular maintenance (painting, repairing woodwork) and some plants need regular pruning.

7. **Costs** € €

8. **No regret:** Yes

107 Green parking lot pergolas, Siedlung Schüngelberg, Gelsenkirchen, Germany

Green Car Parks

1. **General information** The aforementioned planted shadow elements in combination with parking spaces can also be 'stacked up', thus forming a vertical 'parking park'. The walls are replaced with 'plant curtains' and, aside from the parking decks, the building itself doesn't have much thermal mass. This, plus the plants shading, ensure minimal heating. To guarantee sufficient daylight intrusion in winter as well, it is advisable to plant the structure with deciduous plants.

   Depending on the height of the building, you can use climbing plants rooting in the soil (with or without support). If the building is taller than two storeys, you have to work with plant containers planted with climbers or hanging plants. Closed 'green walls' are not a good idea, since these strongly reduce ventilation.

2. **Effectiveness** There is maximum shading on the lower levels. On the upper level, pergola constructions can offer good shading for cars as well.

3. **Extra advantages** Such constructions have a few extra advantages compared to classic car parks. The lower levels are cool and well protected against weather influences. The leaves of the plant constructions also retain particulates. Such a vertical 'parking park' can also be a very special building, which could be used for other purposes too.

4. **Disadvantages** Trees parked under pergolas on the top floor can have blossoms; leaves and fruit fall on them. Animals living in the plants can be nuisances because of their droppings (e.g. birds, plant lice). The more open parts offer less rain protection than closed roofs do.

5. **Construction** Professionals have to plan and build such green car parks.

6. **Maintenance** The maintenance of the building is relatively intensive. Besides normal building upkeep, all climbing

108 *Green car park on top of shops, Miami Beach, Florida, USA*

constructions for the plants have to be maintained. The plants have to be pruned very regularly to ensure safety.

7. Costs € € € €

8. No regret: Yes

Influencing
Reflection

Roofs with High Albedo

1. **General information** When there are heat-sensitive functions right beneath the roofs (such as living or working), it is useful to apply light-coloured materials or 'cool coatings'. There are different types of reflecting roofing materials: from white glazed tiles to metal plates with special coatings. For example: a traditional tile has an albedo of around 0.10-0.35; but painted white, the albedo is 0.75. Another example: the albedo of a roof with corrugated iron sheets is around 0.10-0.15; but painted with a 'cool coating', more than twice the radiation is reflected.

2. **Effectiveness** In summer, a black roof surface can easily have a peak temperature of 80 °C. A white roof, by contrast, can be 17 °C cooler on average. Thanks to reflection, less heat comes into the indoor spaces.

3. **Extra advantages** Because of the moderated temperature fluctuations of the reflecting roofs, the roofing materials suffer less stress. A reflecting roof will therefore have a longer lifespan than a black roof.

4. **Disadvantages** When the white roofs become dirty over time, they will be less effective. The radiation reflected back into the urban canopy layer's air masses can enhance urban heat effects.

5. **Construction** Especially if you are building a new roof or replacing an old one, it makes sense to use reflecting materials or coatings.

6. **Maintenance** For sustained reflection, white roofs have to be cleaned regularly.

7. **Costs** € €

8. **No regret:** Yes

109 *White roof on the M museum in Leuven, Belgium*

Facades with High Albedo

1. **General information** When the indoor climate of a building has to be cooled, the facades can be given a reflecting colour. This way, the wall will absorb less heat, and the rooms behind the walls will not warm up further. The albedo of a classic brick wall is 0.20-0.40 and that of a concrete wall is 0.10-0.35. White paint brings up the albedo to 0.50-0.90.
2. **Effectiveness** Higher albedos result in considerably lower facade surface temperatures. A dark outer wall can easily be 8 to 10 °C warmer than a light one. The over-heating in indoor spaces behind these walls can be reduced by 40-80 per cent of the heat-hours.
3. **Extra advantages** Light coloured facades or parts of facades can sometimes form a special accentuation in the facade design.
4. **Disadvantages** The radiation on objects or people in adjacent street spaces can be increased. So passers-by can become extra warm, which may be unpleasant in the summer. Light facades can become dirty more quickly than dark facades.
5. **Construction** Replacing facade-materials can be complicated, but painting them in a lighter colour is a simple, fast and cheap solution for raising a facade's albedo.
6. **Maintenance** Cleaning or painting once in a while is sufficient for keeping up the albedo.
7. **Costs** € (painting) to € € (replacing facade-material)
8. **No regret:** No

110 *White facades of apartment buildings in Salzburg, Austria*

Surfacing with High Albedo

1. **General information** When large, open, surfaced areas such as squares and outdoor car parks absorb much heat, lighter and smoother materials can be used to reflect incoming radiation and temper the heating. For example: if black asphalt surfaces become so hot in summer that it is uncomfortable to walk on them; or if the asphalt softens and becomes a source of danger to traffic, it is advisable to use materials with a higher albedo. On low-traffic squares, light stones, concrete tiles or clinkers are preferred. Asphalt is the preferred material for parking lots, because it is one of the few materials with the right characteristics for heavy traffic. To make the asphalt lighter in colour, lighter types of added substances can be used. Nowadays, there are alternative new, light-coloured substances to replace the bituminous parts of asphalt, such as NaturalPAVE® or CreaPhalt®.

2. **Effectiveness** The effect of lowering the surface temperature through higher albedos is good. On warm days, concrete surfaces with a lighter colour, for instance, can have a surface temperature that is 20 °C lower than asphalt surfaces.

3. **Extra advantages** None

4. **Disadvantages** Surfaces with a light colour become dirty more quickly and lose some of their reflectivity when they do. On sunny days, light colours can reflect the bright sun in an unpleasant way, and blinding can pose a danger to traffic.

5. **Construction** When public spaces are redeveloped, a lighter surfacing can be chosen. Or when asphalt roads need resurfacing, other additives can be used in the top layer. Specialists have to be involved in the construction.

111 *Light natural stone surfacing, Hightech Campus Eindhoven, the Netherlands*

6. Maintenance For sustained reflection, light coloured surfacing has to be cleaned regularly. The top layer of asphalt can be replaced with a lighter layer during regular maintenance.

7. Costs € € €

8. No regret: No

Outdoor Furniture with High or Low Albedos

1. **General information** The thermal comfort of people in outdoor spaces can depend on the materials they are in direct contact with. Think especially of outdoor furniture people sit on, lean against or even lie down on. When dark surfaces become too hot in summer, for instance, people are not likely to sit on them. In spring or autumn on the other hand, it is nice to sit on a 'preheated' bench. So if you design outdoor furniture, you have to consider when people will use it and adjust the albedo to its use.

2. **Effectiveness** Depending on the albedo, the surface temperature is clearly increased or decreased.

3. **Extra advantages** Furniture with a pleasant surface temperature also creates an inviting ambiance.

4. **Disadvantages** None

5. **Construction** Whether you need professionals to make and place the furniture depends on its size and shape.

6. **Maintenance** The maintenance is highly dependent on the used materials and the shape of the furniture.

7. **Costs** €

8. **No regret:** Yes

112 *Light mosaic bench in Barcelona, Spain*

Influencing Emissivity and Heat Conductivity

'Cool' Walls

1. **General information** Facade-materials with a lower mass are a good solution for keeping the longwave radiation in outdoor spaces of densely built up residential areas as low as possible to prevent enhanced heat island effects. Think of hollow building bricks, aerated concrete, improved insulation or even clay walls. To prevent the outer shell from absorbing heat because of a dark colour, lighter colours should be preferred..

2. **Effectiveness** Depending on the chosen material, heat radiation is clearly reduced.

3. **Extra advantages** Porous materials always have a good insulating effect in indoor spaces.

4. **Disadvantages** None

5. **Construction** The use of these materials is recommended for new residential areas. For existing buildings, changing the outer shell often is not an option. The building constructions often consist of materials emitting much heat, such as bricks or concrete. It is not easy to replace or cover these materials with extra materials. Sometimes the constructions are not suitable, and sometimes it is undesirable for aesthetic reasons, as in the case of historical decorative brickwork that should not be covered.

6. **Maintenance** The maintenance is minimal.

7. **Costs** € €

8. **No regret:** Yes

113 *Woodwork facades, Kop van Zuid, Rotterdam, the Netherlands*

'Heat Emitting' Walls

1. **General information** It can be nice to have some outdoor locations that offer thermal comfort in the cooler seasons. To this end, a high mass wall that retains the scarce warmth can be an advantage. This works best with walls facing south, since these receive the strongest solar radiation for the longest time of the day. Old houses sometimes have benches in front of the facades with the best sun orientation. These benches were a nice place to sit, making use of the direct solar radiation. But even when the sun had gone, the wall's warmth would allow people to sit there a while longer. Not just the walls of buildings, but also walls demarcating plots can function as 'heat emitting walls'.

2. **Effectiveness** On a small scale, the emitted warmth is very effective, but it depends on the building material the wall is made of.

3. **Extra advantages** A wall in a special heat storing material can also be a special touch in the architecture.

4. **Disadvantages** To prevent further warming of a city, it is not advantageous to use these walls in many new buildings. It is better to place 'warm walls' on a small number of carefully chosen spots to create a few warm outdoor public places.

5. **Construction** In principle, such wall elements should be part of the original construction of a new building or demarcation, and professionals should build them.

6. **Maintenance** These walls require minimal maintenance.

7. **Costs** € €

8. **No regret:** No

114 *Built-in wall-seats in Madrid, Spain*

Low-Density Surfacing

1. **General information** If you want surfaces to emit as little longwave radiation as possible, it seems like a good solution to use lower-density materials conducting less heat. But because streets and roads often have to be strong enough to support heavy traffic, you can hardly ever use these lightweight and porous materials. It is, however, possible to use porous materials such as wood or rubber tiles around houses, for terraces and garden paths and such.

2. **Effectiveness** Compared to asphalt, these surfaces can have a significant heat storage and conductivity. Compared to water permeable ground covers with possible vegetation (see page 173), however, the effect of these materials is much smaller.

3. **Extra advantages** Materials such as wood can be of special aesthetic value.

4. **Disadvantages** You can only use these materials on roads and paths with light traffic.

5. **Construction** Professionals have to plan and construct these types of surfacing. Wooden surfaces normally become slippery over time and have to be given an extra coating in areas with much circulation.

6. **Maintenance** Porous surfaces have to be cleaned regularly, and wooden surfaces require regular damage and safety checks.

7. **Costs** € €

8. **No regret:** No

115 Example of a wooden deck, Vondelparc, Utrecht, the Netherlands

Low-Conductivity Outdoor Furniture

1. **General information** The materials used for outdoor furniture can have a strong influence on people's thermal comfort upon touch. In cold circumstances, fast-conducting materials such as metals can subtract heat from the body so fast that the skin can freeze on to it. In warm circumstances, they can become so hot as to cause light burns. So it is important to select materials attuned to people's thermal sensation. In general, it is best to use materials such as wood, plastic or porous stone, because of their low conductivity.
2. **Effectiveness** The use of low-conductivity outdoor furniture has a clear effect on the people using it. The material is nice to touch, since it does not subtract extra warmth from the skin or subject it to extra heat.
3. **Extra advantages** These materials usually also give a 'warm', inviting ambiance to outdoor spaces.
4. **Disadvantages** None
5. **Construction** Depending on the type and construction, making outdoor furniture can be quite simple or really craftsman's work.
6. **Maintenance** Wooden furniture may need more upkeep (paint, stain) than plastic furniture. Porous stone has to be cleaned regularly.
7. **Costs** €
8. **No regret:** Yes

116 *Wooden bench, Parque de Manzanares, Madrid, Spain*

Influencing
Evaporation

Intensive and Irrigated Green Roofs

1. General information Nowadays, people generally see green roofs as *the* solution to the urban heat problem. But there are one or two things to be said about this. The cooling effect depends on how thick the substrate is; the vegetation's leaf-surfaces and the level of irrigation. Extensive roofs such as sedum roofs often do not have cooling effect through evaporation. Intensive green roofs with a lot of vegetation, on the other hand, can contribute to cooling. An intensive green roof has a thick substrate layer of at least 25 centimetres for perennials, 40 centimetres for shrubbery and over 80 centimetres for trees.

2. Effectiveness Because of the plants' shadows, the surface temperature during peak hours is easily about 20 °C lower than that of conventional roofs. Measurements taken in New York show that the surface temperature of well-watered green roofs is just as low or lower than that of white roofs. On the hottest time of the day, the surface temperature of the green roof was an impressive 33 °C lower than that of a black roof. Green roofs can be a way to lower the heat island effect, but in order to do so, they have to be used on the largest possible scale. People should also be aware that the cooling effect mostly concerns the area above the roofs and not people's everyday environment that is situated in the streets. That is why generally speaking green roofs are not as effective for the urban climate as people say they are.

3. Extra advantages If, besides cooling the surroundings, you also want to efficiently lower temperatures indoors and thus be able to use less air conditioning, intensive roofs are recommended. The insulation of the substrate layer provides cooling, which can mean around 5 °C lower indoor temperatures right beneath the roof. Eventually, this can

117 *Intensive roof park, Köln Arcaden, Cologne, Germany*

result in around 25 per cent yearly savings on energy costs for air conditioning. Intensive roof gardens are pleasant outdoor areas, which can be seen as extra living space. When intensive roofs are combined with photovoltaic elements, this installation works more efficiently because of the extra cooling of the plants underneath.

4. Disadvantages None

5. Construction Because of the high pressure load, intensive green roofs need strong bearing constructions. Therefore, it usually is not possible to use these roofs on existing buildings. The construction of new buildings has to be calculated for the extra weight on the roof.

6. Maintenance Intensive green roofs require quite a lot of maintenance (checking them about eight times a year, weeding, et cetera), plus they need irrigation in dry periods.

7. Costs € € €

8. No regret: Yes

'Water Roofs and Walls'

1. **General information** For cooling the insides of buildings, but also for cooling closed outdoor spaces, you can consider 'water roofs and water walls'. Think of using nozzles or water films to keep roofs or other building surfaces moist; or of storing water on a flat roof with a cover over it. These techniques were already used in old Indian palaces. The cooled air from a water roof was lead into the indoor spaces of these palaces. So it is an ancient technique that can still be of use today.

2. **Effectiveness** Storing water on roofs can lead to 10 to 20 °C lower surface temperatures (air temperatures to a lesser degree) and inside to around 5 °C lower temperatures. On walls, surface temperature reductions up to 10 °C have been measured when water films were applied.

3. **Extra advantages** Water roofs can play an important role in buffering peak rainfalls.

4. **Disadvantages** None

5. **Construction** Watering vertical building surfaces usually requires many technical installations, but storing water on flat roofs is a relatively easy thing to plan for new buildings. The building construction has to be strong enough to support the extra weight of the water, though. Planning and construction has to be left to experts.

6. **Maintenance** The installations have to be cleaned and checked regularly.

7. **Costs** € € €

8. **No regret:** Yes

118 *'Water wall', Floriade 2002, Haarlemmermeer, the Netherlands*

Low Plants

1. **General information** Many front and back gardens are paved these days – with many negative consequences for the radiation balance and the indoor and outdoor climate. For this reason, it is better to use lower plants that do not cast shadows on the house. Think of vegetation such as grass, perennial plants, flowers, vegetables and moss. With their evapotranspiration, the plants will contribute to a tempered air temperature.

2. **Effectiveness** Naturally, smaller plants have lower evapotranspiration than large plants, since they have less foliage. But because these plants usually grow in the earth, we can add the evaporation from the soil. Especially moss can evaporate much water when the water supply from the soil is continuous.

3. **Extra advantages** Low vegetation is important for the biodiversity in a city, and it usually has an aesthetic effect too. Lawns can also be used for many recreational activities. Urban agriculture falls into this category as well, and many of these areas have an important educational and social function besides the production of food.

4. **Disadvantages** When lawns become parched, they stop cooling and can have the opposite effect on the urban climate. Planting larger trees can partially prevent this problem, since their shadows help put a stop to yellowing.

5. **Construction** Much low vegetation in the city doesn't need to be planted. It grows on its own, for instance in brownfield areas. Planting lawns, gardens and perennial beds isn't very

119 *Informal urban agriculture in Overtown, Miami, USA*

difficult, and only very sophisticated planting schemes require the work of professional gardeners.

6. Maintenance The maintenance depends on the type of low vegetation and the intensity of use. A brownfield doesn't require any and an extensive bed only a little maintenance, whereas intensive perennials, vegetables and lawns need a lot of attention (mowing, weeding, et cetera).

7. Costs 0 - €

8. No regret: Yes

Waterfalls

1. **General information** On warm days, cool spots with flowing water in parks are very popular places to stay. If brooks run through these parks and the relief allows for it, waterfalls can be constructed. The falling motion spreads the water in fine drops, resulting in high evaporation and a lower local air temperature.
2. **Effectiveness** This evaporation and thus tempering of the air temperature is reasonably effective.
3. **Extra advantages** A waterfall is a special addition to a park and a magnet for playing children.
4. **Disadvantages** None
5. **Construction** Professionals have to plan and construct waterfalls.
6. **Maintenance** None
7. **Costs** € €
8. **No regret:** Yes

120 *Waterfalls of the Ovato fountains in Villa d'Este, Tivoli, Italy*

Graduation Works

1. **General information** Graduation works (or thorn houses) are a special way to evaporate water. These installations were already built centuries ago to evaporate salty water and win the salt. Graduation works consist of a vertical construction with a netting of fine twigs (usually hawthorn) on which water falls. The netting refines the water into smaller drops, so it evaporates faster. Spas also use these graduation works to seep mineral water over it, so guests can breathe in the minerals with the water vapour. The graduation works' surroundings are full of small water drops that can evaporate quickly and thus cool the air considerably. When there is sufficient natural relief, graduation works can be used without extra pumps.
2. **Effectiveness** The evaporation and thus tempering of the air temperature is very effective.
3. **Extra advantages** Graduation works are a special addition to a space and are of great experiential value.
4. **Disadvantages** None
5. **Construction** Experienced experts have to plan and construct graduation works.
6. **Maintenance** The netting has to be replaced regularly, which is very specialist work.
7. **Costs** € €
8. **No regret:** Yes

121 *Graduation works in Revierpark Mattlerbusch, Duisburg, Germany*

'Green Ponds'

1. **General information** Water bodies generally are not very effective when it comes to lowering the air temperature, but if they are planted with dense vegetation or, for example, Spaghnum mosses, the plants evaporate much water. The plants' shadows also cool the water surface. Together, water and plants are a workable option for controlling the air temperature.

2. **Effectiveness** Scientists measured the air temperature around rice fields in Tokyo. These measurements showed that the decrease in air temperature above the fields and up to 150 metres distance on the leeward side was still 2 °C; which is a considerable effect.

3. **Extra advantages** Green ponds can buffer rainwater and improve biodiversity. You can also think of a combination with helophyte-filter functions.

4. **Disadvantages** Prolonged periods of heat can cause problems with blue-green algae if the water is stagnant.

5. **Construction** Laypeople can construct small green ponds. Professionals best construct larger ponds or ponds with technically more complicated overflow systems.

6. **Maintenance** The maintenance is relatively minimal. To prevent paedogenesis, one should clear out the vegetation regularly.

7. **Costs** € - € €

8. **No regret:** Yes

122 *A green pond*

Fountains

1. **General information** On paved squares without natural evaporation through the soil, the humidity has to be increased in other ways. The most obvious and traditional solution is a fountain. Fountains come in all shapes and sizes, but for effective cooling of the surroundings, a fountain ideally spreads the most possible water in the smallest possible drops over a large space. The *giochi d'aqua* (water games) in historical gardens are an early example of cooling through evaporation on a small scale.

2. **Effectiveness** A study of a larger fountain in Japan (with about 2 metres high pillars from which water flows and is finely sprayed out) showed a decrease in temperature on the leeside of the fountain of around 3 °C. The cooling effect of the fountain could be felt up to 35 metres from the fountain.

3. **Extra advantages** Fountains also have an important aesthetic value and invite people to paddle; children love playing with water.

4. **Disadvantages** The water installations require very careful maintenance; otherwise there can be problems with pathogens such as legionella.

5. **Construction** The planning and construction of a fountain with spray pumps for fine water drops is specialists' work.

6. **Maintenance** Fountains need to be checked-up, cleaned and maintained regularly.

7. **Costs** € €

8. **No regret:** Yes

123 *Fountain with fine water spray, Parc Charles de Gaulle, Paris, France*

Water Mist Installations

1. **General information** New techniques allow for very fine mist sprays. These mists contain such fine water particles that, for the most part, these are evaporated even before they precipitate as water drops on surfaces or people in the surroundings of the installations. There are several types of water mist installations. They can be freestanding and function like a sort of shower. They can also be integrated in half-open spaces, for instance in so-called 'cooling towers'; where the mist is sprayed in cylinder-shaped coverings at the top, evaporates along the way down, and arrives at ground level as cool air.

2. **Effectiveness** Water mist installations are exceptionally effective when it comes to cooling the air. Measurements done at a cooling tower when it was 41 °C outside, showed an air temperature of 24 °C at the bottom of the tower – a huge difference in temperature! The evaporation is not the only reason for this difference, though; the tower's shadow also plays a part. Freestanding water mist installations without shading are less effective, but they are still a very good at cooling the air.

3. **Extra advantages** With distinctive designs, these installations can be a beautiful addition to public spaces.

4. **Disadvantages** The water mist installations require very careful maintenance; otherwise there can be problems with pathogens such as legionella.

5. **Construction** Specialists should do the planning and construction of water mist installations.

6. **Maintenance** Water mist installations need to be checked-up, cleaned and maintained very regularly.

7. **Costs** € €

8. **No regret:** Yes

124 *A mist shower in a shopping mall in California, USA*

'Greening Masts'

1. **General information** If there is not enough room in streets to plant trees, an alternative is to have plants grow up masts to temper the air temperature through evapotranspiration.
2. **Effectiveness** The effect is clearly less than that of a fully-grown tree, but it is still significant.
3. **Extra advantages** Birds and insects can find a home in the green masts. These masts can be a special addition to the street profile.
4. **Disadvantages** For maintenance of the masts themselves, the climbing plants have to be largely removed.
5. **Construction** Very simple: all you usually have to do is remove the hard surface around the masts and plant robust climbers.
6. **Maintenance** The maintenance is minimal, the plants might have to be pruned **once in a while, especially with lampposts.**
7. **Costs** €
8. **No regret:** No

125 *Green masts in Kassel, Germany*

'De-paving' areas

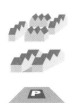

1. **General information** Cities have many paved surfaces that retain heat. To temper the air temperature, de-paving and making places green is therefore a big improvement. Hard surfaces should best be kept to a minimum and only be used when there is no alternative. All other places can be covered with gravel or vegetation. Well-known solutions such as green banks, green parking lots and green tram rails can be used much more often. Low-traffic streets can get a minimal paving of 'cart tracks' in grass or with grass tiles.

2. **Effectiveness** Removing the surfacing in itself already results in better evaporation of the soil's moisture. Add vegetation, and you get the evapotranspiration of the plants as well, adding to the cooling effect.

3. **Extra advantages** Removing surfacing adds to the biodiversity in cities. Open ground is better for water buffering. When the paving of traffic lanes is reduced to a minimum, the adjacent vegetation can filter fine dust particles from the traffic at their source. The construction of minimal surfacing often makes the construction of extra water drainage systems superfluous, since the water can seep directly into the soil.

4. **Disadvantages** Gravel pavement can erode with time and can get silted up with fine particles, thus reducing the water permeability.

5. **Construction** De-paving and placing gravel and grass tiles and such have to be carefully planned. In public spaces this should be done by professionals.

6. **Maintenance** To guarantee permeability, gravel has to be maintained or replaced regularly. The plants growing on or in the permeable surface have to be mowed and/or weeded.

7. **Costs** € €

8. **No regret:** Yes

126 *Green tram rails in The Hague, the Netherlands*

Sprinkling Streets

1. **General information** Sprinkling is a good alternative for cooling paved traffic spaces where none of the aforementioned installations can be placed. Especially in Mediterranean countries, streets and sidewalks are often sprayed with water, and this is an old tradition in Japan as well – the *uchimizu*. This sprinkling can be done by hand or automatically through small, built-in nozzles in the street or the curb that are connected to the water network. Some countries, such as France, now have automatic systems.

2. **Effectiveness** This method seems most effective in the morning and late afternoon in direct sunlight. Sprinkling 1 litre per square metre every 30 minutes, decreases the surface temperature with 2-4 °C.

3. **Extra advantages** The sprinkling also binds dust particles in the street. Sprinkler systems can be combined with saltwater-sprinklers against snow and ice.

4. **Disadvantages** The sprinkler systems are sensitive.

5. **Construction** Planning and constructing sprinkler systems is very specialized work.

6. **Maintenance** The sprinkler systems need regular check-ups and cleaning to prevent blockage.

7. **Costs** € for manual sprinkling to € € € for nozzle systems.

8. **No regret:** Yes

127 *Street sprinklers in Lyon, France*

Slowing or Avoiding Wind

Orientation of Large Freestanding Buildings

1. **General information** For large, freestanding buildings, it is better to avoid orientations at right angles or at an angle with the wind. An orientation parallel to the wind is preferable.

2. **Effectiveness** For the outdoor areas in front of and along the sides of the building, the effect is very clear, because corner streams and downwash effects are minimized.

3. **Construction** You have to plan the construction of a building with a different wind orientation well, and you have to adjust the layout of the building to it, for example to guarantee optimal sunlight schemes for the rooms.

4. **Maintenance** Depends on the building.

5. **Costs** Depend on the building.

128 *Avoid orientation of large buildings at right angles to the wind and prefer orientations parallel to the wind*

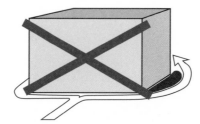
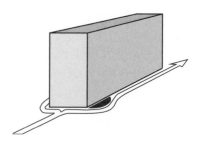

Wind Protection around Tall Buildings

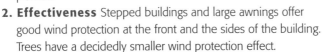

1. **General information** Pedestrians, cyclists and other users of areas around tall buildings (of over 20 metres tall) have to be protected against downwash. Wind protection should preferably be placed in or on the building itself. This can be achieved through the use of gradually smaller building volumes, but also with elements such as awnings. These elements deflect downwash winds before they reach the pedestrian level. Alternatively, big 'tree packages' can be planted.

2. **Effectiveness** Stepped buildings and large awnings offer good wind protection at the front and the sides of the building. Trees have a decidedly smaller wind protection effect.

3. **Construction** The construction of a stepped building or a building with awnings requires proper planning and the building's floor plan has to be adjusted to it. The 'steps' of podium-shaped buildings can be used as an extra indoor space. The precise location of tree planting has to be carefully planned, but planting them is relatively simple, providing the soil circumstances are good and there is sufficient rooting space.

4. **Maintenance** This depends on the type of wind protection and the size of the building.

5. **Costs** This depends on the type of wind protection and the size of the building.

129 Tall buildings with awnings, a stepped shape or 'tree packages' to deflect downwash

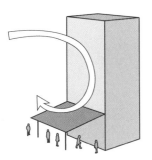
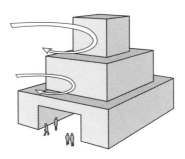
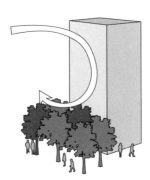

Avoiding Outdoor Functions in Narrowed Spaces

1. **General information** When large buildings (over 20 metres tall and over 30 metres wide) are provided with underpasses or passages, or if they stand close together, draught situations occur in these narrowed spaces, which makes them unsuitable as locations to stay outdoors. With very large building volumes this can even lead to wind danger, depending on the prevailing wind direction. Pedestrian and bicycle routes then have to be relocated to places without wind danger.
2. **Effectiveness** Not applicable
3. **Construction** Not applicable
4. **Maintenance** Not applicable
5. **Costs** Not applicable

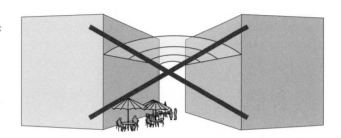

130 *Avoid outdoor functions in narrowed spaces*

Windbreaks (with Trees)

1. **General information** To protect gardens against wind nuisance or to protect houses from too much wind, fences or vegetation (hedges or trees with denser foliage) can deflect the wind around the buildings or the areas that are to be protected. It doesn't really matter if the windbreak is a built object or if it consists of vegetation. The density of the windbreak determines how effective it is (see illustration 131).

2. **Effectiveness** In general, windbreaks can be quite effective. How porous the fence or vegetation is plays an important role in this. When a windbreak is only a little porous, there will be a small, but very sheltered area on the leeside of it. When a windbreak is more porous, the wind protection on the leeside is not as strong as it would be behind a closed obstacle, but the sheltered area behind the windbreak is much larger. With fences, the shape and direction of the boarding also plays a role (see illustration 132). The illustrations show the effect of different windbreak porosities on the wind behind it.

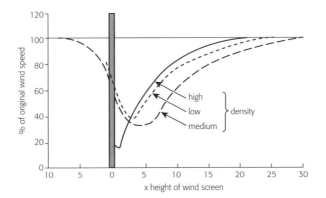

131 *Densities of windbreaks and the sheltered effect behind them*

132 *Windbreaks with different boarding and their effect on the wind patterns behind them*

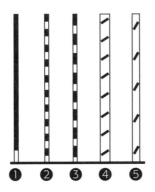

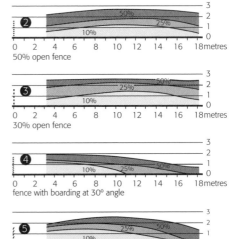

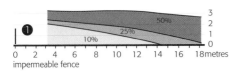

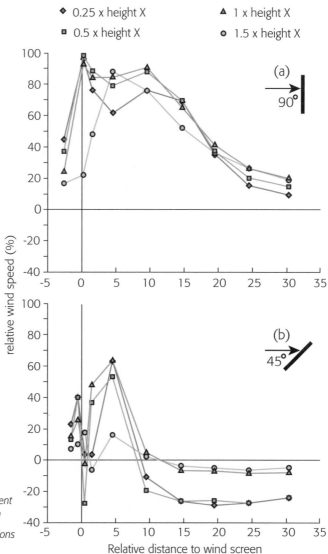

133 *Windbreaks of different heights, and angles and their wind speed reductions*

The optimal wind protection is obtained when windbreaks are at right angles to the wind direction. As soon as the position of the windbreak is shifted so that it is no longer at right angles to the direction of the wind, its protection directly behind the object is reduced, and further back it even has a reversed effect (see illustration 133).

If you place several windbreaks at right angles to the wind direction at the end of the protected zone of the windbreak in front, an extra wind speed reduction of around 10 per cent can be achieved.

3. **Construction** The planning of windbreaks, hedgerows and dense tree plantings has to be well thought-out. Planting hedges and trees is relatively easy, but wind-protecting fences usually have to be made and placed by professionals.

4. Maintenance The maintenance depends on the type of windbreak. Wooden windbreaks have to be painted once in a while. Windbreaks made from other materials such as metal, glass or plastic require less upkeep. Hedges have to be pruned regularly and windbreaks with trees need relatively little care.

5. Costs Depending on the type of windbreak, the costs vary between € and € €.

Changing Street Orientation

1. **General information** When streets are parallel to the direction of the most frequent and strong winds, the wind can easily be 'channelled', and you can expect problems with wind nuisance. On many days of the year, there will be too much wind for people to sit outside comfortably, and stronger winds can also be dangerous to pedestrians and cyclists. This will certainly be an issue if taller buildings flank the streets. These problems can only be solved with changes in the street orientation, especially if you want to invite people to walk or cycle through these streets.

2. **Effectiveness** For optimal countering of the wind channelling, the street's orientation should change after ten to twenty times the average building height.

3. **Construction** Changing the orientation of streets should be planned carefully, because later interventions in the urban tissue will be less effective. So these measures are possible for new streets and mainly for streets with little traffic. These measures are less recommendable for streets with heavy and high-speed traffic, since abrupt changes of street directions hinder traffic flows.

4. **Maintenance** Not applicable

5. **Costs** Not applicable

134 *Streets with alternating orientations have less wind nuisance*

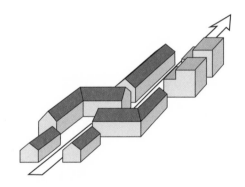

Street Trees Against Channelling Effect

1. **General information** In existing streets, wind nuisance caused by the channelling effect often has to be overcome. But you can't simply change all the adjacent buildings. In such cases, planting street trees can help, because tree crowns softly swirl the wind and thus weaken it.

2. **Effectiveness** This measure is not as effective as the construction of streets with changing orientations is, but it is still considerable. It is important not to plant the trees too close together, because then they could form such a closed volume, that they can cause their own channelling effect. Trees planted too close together can also form a 'green tunnel', inducing accumulation of fine dust particles.

3. **Construction** Professionals should be the ones to plant trees in streets, because they often have to prepare specific planting sites with systems for aeration and irrigation.

4. **Maintenance** Street trees often need more care than trees in parks or outside cities because they are faced with more stress factors (heat, drought, road salt). They also have to be pruned and their leaves have to be cleaned up.

5. **Costs** € - € €

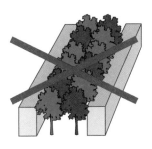

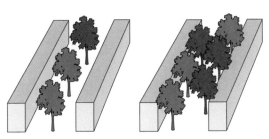

135 *Street trees reducing the channelling effect, but not yet forming a 'green tunnel'*

'Wind-Optimized' Squares

1. General information For a comfortable climate in squares, controlling the wind is of the utmost importance. The designs of squares have to adapt the proportions of the open space and the orientation to the prevailing wind to each other. Especially in windy regions, squares should not be too wide. A rule of thumb for good square proportions regarding wind is based on the relation between square surface and the surrounding building heights. This rule has a simple formula: square surface / average height of surrounding buildings x 2 = < 6. The designers can play with the building heights and/or the size of the square surface to arrive at the right proportions.

When a square has openings at its edges (e.g. street entrances) taking up over 25 per cent of the square perimeter, this usually results in too high wind speeds across the square. It is therefore better not to have the openings exceed this 25 per cent. It is also better to avoid situating large openings in the prevailing wind direction. When squares have an oblong shape parallel to the prevailing wind direction, a channelling effect will occur. Ideally, oblong squares for outdoor functions have an orientation perpendicular to the prevailing wind. If this is not an option, setting back some of the surrounding buildings can improve the situation. On oblong squares parallel to the wind direction that also taper to a narrower space, the air is compressed even more. Wind-sensitive functions should be avoided on such places in the squares.

136 *Diagram of all 'ideal characteristics' of a wind-friendly square*

2. Effectiveness We can expect truly improved wind climates when squares are designed with these guidelines in mind.

3. Construction The opportunity to design a square from

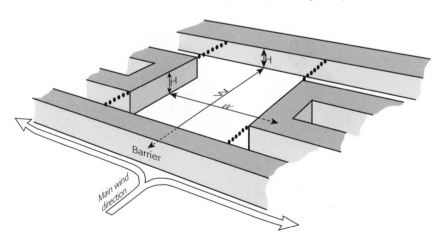

•••••• Open perimeter should be <25% total perimeter

H/W   ratios should be > 0.3

scratch does not often present itself, because the largest part of the urban tissue is already there. The shapes of the surrounding buildings of existing squares generally cannot be altered. You then have to go for smaller or less 'radical' solutions (see following solutions).

4. Maintenance Not applicable

5. Costs Not applicable

'Ring of Trees'

1. **General information** On squares that are too wide, a ring of trees along the edges of the square can make the open space smaller. This decreases the area for the wind to pick up speed.

2. **Effectiveness** A ring of trees is obviously less effective than improved square proportions, but trees also have many other advantages for the urban climate and biodiversity and have experiential value.

3. **Construction** Planting trees in squares should be done by professionals, because they often have to prepare specific planting sites with systems for aeration and irrigation.

4. **Maintenance** Trees on squares often need more care than trees in parks or outside cities because they are faced with more stress factors (heat, drought, road salt). They also have to be pruned and their leaves have to be cleaned up.

5. **Costs** € €

137 *Ring of trees around het Plein, The Hague, the Netherlands*

Urban Shelterbelt

1. **General information** When specific larger parts of a square have to be protected, you can think of a special kind of windbreak: a treeline with semi-permeable windscreens placed in the trunk space, a combination I call an 'urban shelterbelt'. Ideally, the windscreens are mobile, so room can be made for pedestrians, cyclists, and loading and unloading goods for markets and such.
2. **Effectiveness** The area behind an urban shelterbelt that is well protected from the wind is usually twice as long as the height of the trees. For medium-sized trees of 20 metres tall, for example, there is around 40 metres of space behind the urban shelterbelt where wind speeds are halved.
3. **Construction** Professionals have to design and place the windscreens and plant the trees on squares. For the trees, they often have to prepare specific planting sites with systems for aeration and irrigation.
4. **Maintenance** Trees on squares often need more care than trees in parks or outside of cities because they are faced with more stress factors (heat, drought, road salt). They also have to be pruned and their leaves have to be cleaned up. The windscreens have to be checked, cleaned and maintained regularly, especially if they have moving parts.
5. **Costs** € € €

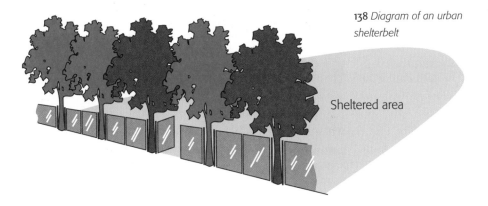

138 Diagram of an urban shelterbelt

Sheltered area

Windscreens on Windy Places

1. **General information** There are many places that need small-scale local wind protection because people want to stay there, for instance on sidewalk cafés. These windy places can be located at the spots where streets come onto squares, on waterfronts or in open squares. These places then have to be provided with small and possibly flexible solutions for wind protection. In all cases you have to find out how the wind flows and preferably place windscreens at right angles to the wind. In many European countries, large beer breweries offer free windscreens to bar owners. Place-specific and specially designed windscreens, however, are rare. A real opportunity for designers!

2. **Effectiveness** The effectiveness of the windscreens depends on their porosity and size (see 'Windbreaks', page 179).

3. **Construction** Flexible windscreens are easy to put up. Fixed windscreens on the other hand, have to be installed by professionals.

4. **Maintenance** Occasional cleaning or painting the windscreens and oiling the moving parts are usually all the maintenance windscreens require.

5. **Costs** €

139 *Windscreen on a street corner in Salzburg, Austria*

Wind Protective Street Furniture

1. **General information** When there is no room on squares for large-scale wind protection, small wind protected places on the street level itself can be provided as an alternative. Think of furniture with integrated windscreens, as we sometimes see on coastal boulevards, or of benches combined with a hedge. We can also imagine special solutions that can address the problem when the wind comes from different directions: swivelling sheltered seats. For example: a high-backed bench, which functions as a windscreen, with a sail to turn it, so that the bench is always sheltered from the wind.
2. **Effectiveness** For people sitting on the bench, this is very effective, but beyond the seat itself, this type of street furniture has no effect.
3. **Construction** Professionals have to design and place this specially designed street furniture, especially if it is movable.
4. **Maintenance** The maintenance of these elements depends on the materials. Solutions with moving parts require much maintenance.
5. **Costs** € €

140 *Example of a 'sail-bench' that turns, so people sitting on it are always sheltered from the wind*

Ventilation

Ventilation Around Houses

1. **General information** In gardens and on premises around houses, it seems like a good idea to plant as few trees as possible and place as few wind-deflecting objects as possible for ventilation, but this obviously makes no sense. Knowing that wind protection is desirable in all seasons except for the summer, we have to find compromises. High, closed elements around plots could, for example, only be placed where they are needed for wind protection and privacy. In other places, the plot demarcating elements can be partially open or be made of a wide-meshed fence.

2. **Effectiveness** Ventilation options in the garden help improve the ventilation of the garden itself and indirectly of the house. Naturally, optimal placing of the windows and ventilation openings in the architecture itself guarantee good ventilation inside the house.

3. **Construction** The construction depends on the type of plot demarcation element and the type of vegetation.

4. **Maintenance** The maintenance depends on the type of plot demarcation element and the type of vegetation.

5. **Costs** €

141 *Diagram of a half-open plot demarcation at a house*

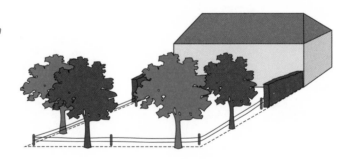

Channelling Cool Airflows

1. **General information** When cooling airflows have to be directed to a certain place, volumes such as buildings, walls, trees and hedges and such can be used. These then have to be configured in such a way that they guide the wind to that place without staggering, because otherwise they guide the wind in undesired directions.
2. **Effectiveness** Channelling can help use the cool airflows more efficiently, but because the airflows are relatively weak, this effect is limited.
3. **Construction** The construction depends on the type of elements used to guide the wind, and these can be very different.
4. **Maintenance** The maintenance depends on the types of elements used.
5. **Costs** Depending on the type of volumes: € - € €

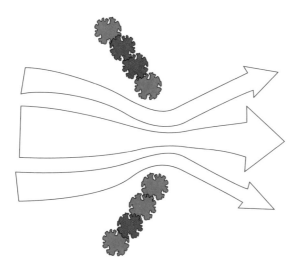

142 *Airflow-guidance by plant volumes*

Designing Protection Against Precipitation

Glass Canopies

1. **General information** The designs of canopies have to ensure sufficient protection against rain. If a canopy is placed too high up, the wind often blows in the rain under it. Rain is generally paired with wind from a typical direction, which you can find out from the data of weather institutes. Canopies that are open in this direction therefore have to be sufficiently wide and not too high, so as to make sure that the rain won't fall on the people underneath.
2. **Effectiveness** With the right orientation, width and height, coverings can be very effective.
3. **Extra advantages** Many canopies can also offer shading, if so desired.
4. **Disadvantages** Glass canopies are sensitive to vandalism.
5. **Construction** The size of the construction, safety requirements and sometimes the technical finesse of the canopies require expert construction.
6. **Maintenance** For the most part, the maintenance consists of painting the supportive constructions and cleaning the glass.
7. **Costs** €
8. **No regret:** Yes

143 *Example of a bad and a good glass canopy*

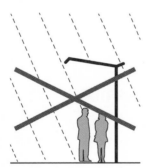
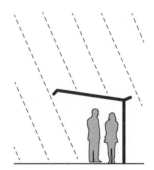

Dome-Shaped Deciduous Trees

1. **General information** Many deciduous trees are also suitable for rain protection, if they have a dense and screen- or dome-shaped crown. In the dark months, the crowns allow for much light, since they have shed their leaves then.
2. **Effectiveness** In the seasons when the trees do have foliage, the leaves can offer good protection against the rain.
3. **Extra advantages** Deciduous trees have numerous other advantages for the urban climate, and also for the biodiversity and an aesthetic value.
4. **Disadvantages** You also need precipitation protection in winter, and trees are much less effective then, since they have shed their foliage.
5. **Construction** It is easy to plant trees in parks. In the paved areas of the city, planting trees requires extra facilities, such as plant holes and possible aeration and irrigation options. Generally speaking, this is work for professional gardeners.
6. **Maintenance** Trees in parks require relatively little care, but trees in paved areas often need more care because they are faced with more stress factors (heat, drought, road salt). The trees sometimes have to be irrigated in hot situations. All trees have to be pruned and their leaves have to be cleaned up.
7. **Costs** 0 - € €
8. **No regret:** Yes

144 *Dome-shaped tree*

Designing for Multiple Microclimate Factors

Waterfall Pergola

1. **General information** When shadow alone does not offer sufficient cooling in hot situations, a shadow element can also be combined with a water element, which provides extra evaporation. This can be a pergola-type, green construction with water splashing down from it.

2. **Effectiveness** The combination of shadow, evaporation from the plants *and* finely sprayed water results in very effective tempering of the air temperature.

3. **Extra advantages** The advantages are a combination of those of a pergola and a fountain. When the construction of the pergola is not too heavy and it is planted with deciduous plants, it allows the sunlight to come through it in winter.

4. **Disadvantages** The water installation can become dirty and there can be problems with pathogens, e.g. legionella.

5. **Construction** Specialists have to do the planning, calculating and construction of these installations.

6. **Maintenance** The maintenance is intensive. The pergola has to be given a paintjob regularly and some plants have to be pruned. The waterfall-part has to be checked and cleaned on a regular basis.

7. **Costs** € €

8. **No regret:** Yes

145 *Pergola with waterfall*

Photochromic Glass Roof

1. **General information** Sometimes places have to be protected from the rain, but also require sufficient light. On sunny days, on the other hand, this place has to be protected from the sun. For such a place, you could think of a glass roof with the same type of photochromic glass used in sunglasses. When the sun is out, the roof becomes dark so that it shades, and when it is cloudy, the roof offers rain protection.
2. **Effectiveness** This installation will be very effective.
3. **Extra advantages** Besides the combination of microclimatic advantages, this installation will let people see changes in the intensity of solar radiation in an interesting way.
4. **Disadvantages** The construction may be sensitive to vandalism.
5. **Construction** Specialists have to develop this element and professionals have to install it.
6. **Maintenance** The glass parts have to be cleaned regularly.
7. **Costs** € € €
8. **No regret:** Yes

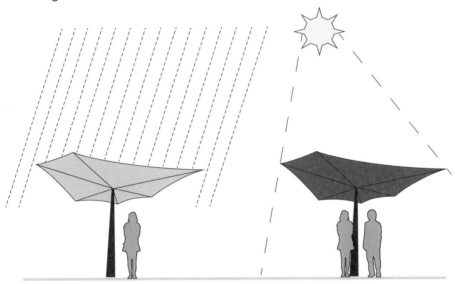

146 *Illustration of the photochromic glass roof when it rains and when it's sunny*

'Parasol / Umbrella'

1. **General information** For a place that needs protection both from rain and from the sun, you can use a large, foldable screen. Users can press a button to open the screen on demand.
2. **Effectiveness** This is an optimal solution for sun and rain protection.
3. **Extra advantages** This installation is a playful element that people in the city can use precisely at those moments when they need it.
4. **Disadvantages** The installation, and especially the textile elements, can be sensitive to vandalism.
5. **Construction** This element should be developed and installed by professionals.
6. **Maintenance** The maintenance will be quite high in order to guarantee the functioning of the moving parts.
7. **Costs** € €
8. **No regret:** Yes

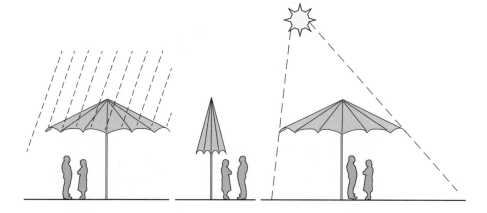

147 *Illustration of the way the parasol/umbrella works*

'Wind plus Shadow' Elements

1. **General information** For locations in need of wind and sun protection, you can combine these functions in one piece of outdoor furniture. For example: a higher element like a plant container or earthen wall can provide seating sheltered from the wind, and the plants in the container can provide shadow.
2. **Effectiveness** Directly behind the element, the wind speed is very effectively reduced. Depending on the density of the plants and the permeability of the foliage, a shadow depth of 50 per cent and over can be achieved.
3. **Extra advantages** Besides having advantages for the microclimate, this option could offer possibilities for more biodiversity.
4. **Disadvantages** None
5. **Construction** In principle, you do not have to be a professional to place these elements. When these are placed in a public space, however, you may have to meet extra safety requirements, and professionals then have to install them.
6. **Maintenance** Depending on the material, the bench has to be maintained. The plants have to be weeded occasionally.
7. **Costs** €
8. **No regret:** Yes

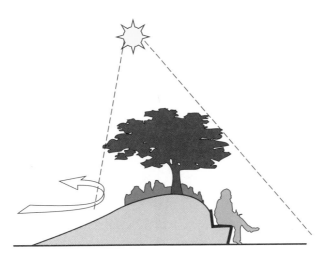

148 *'Mini-dune':
a place with wind
and sun protection*

'Windscreen-Tree-Bench'

1. **General information** Sometimes, you want to create a shaded spot under a tree, but because the tree is freestanding, it can be a little draughty and the wind can come from different directions. For this situation, you can think of a tree-bench with flexible windscreens. The windscreens are placed at right angles to the bench, so the person sitting on the bench is protected from wind coming in from the sides.

2. **Effectiveness** Directly behind the windscreens, the wind is blocked very effectively. Depending on the permeability of the foliage, a shadow depth of 50 per cent can be achieved.

3. **Extra advantages** All other advantages of a tree (cooler air temperature, biodiversity and aesthetical value) hold here as well.

4. **Disadvantages** None

5. **Construction** Since the moving parts of the windscreen form a complicated construction, professionals have to plan and install them. If the trees are planted on squares, specific planting sites with systems for aeration and irrigation may have to be prepared.

4. **Maintenance** Trees on squares often need more care than trees in a park because they are faced with more stress factors (heat, drought, road salt). In hot situations, the trees may require irrigation. They also have to be pruned and their leaves have to be cleaned up. The windscreens with their moving parts have to be checked, cleaned and maintained regularly.

7. **Costs** € €

8. **No regret:** Yes

149 *Illustration of a 'windscreen-tree-bench"*

'Wind-or-Shadow' Screens

1. **General information** The weather circumstances in many countries with a temperate climate feature two typical situations in which protection is needed: when it is cloudy and there is a strong wind, people have to be protected from it. On hot, sunny days, on the other hand, when normally there is not much wind, people need to be shaded. Moveable screens offering protection against the wind or the sun are a simple solution. We can think of systems on various scales, from a seat for one person to protective constructions for several people.

2. **Effectiveness** Because they block wind and sun on a small scale, these elements are very effective.

3. **Extra advantages** With the options for several people, you can get continuously changing screen patterns, playfully revealing the personal comfort needs of the users.

4. **Disadvantages** If the screens are made of textile, the objects are sensitive to vandalism.

5. **Construction** These constructions have to be well planned in advance, and professionals have to build them.

6. **Maintenance** Because of their relatively complicated construction and moving parts, these objects require very regular maintenance.

7. **Costs** € - € €

8. **No regret:** Yes

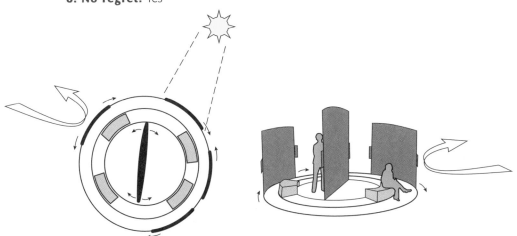

150 *Illustration of interactive 'wind or shadow' screens*

Groundwater-Driven Wind Protection

1. **General information** In areas with relatively high groundwater levels, such as river areas, you can think of a very different solution. In the cooler seasons (spring, autumn and winter), the groundwater level is often high in these areas. The wind is also stronger in these seasons. In the summer, on the other hand, the wind is weaker and the groundwater level is lower. It is possible to design a system of elements moving up and down, driven by the groundwater level and thus offering wind protection. Such a system can consist of, for instance, lightweight pillars, raised and lowered by the changing groundwater level.

2. **Effectiveness** When long rows of these pillars form a sort of wall, these can offer effective wind protection.

3. **Extra advantages** Besides the windscreen function, these pillars playfully indicate the groundwater levels.

4. **Disadvantages** None

5. **Construction** This system requires specialist knowledge of hydrology and engineering, so experts have to do the work.

6. **Maintenance** This installation has to be checked regularly and the maintenance is high, because of the sliding parts and the impact of the groundwater on the construction.

7. **Costs** € €

8. **No regret:** Yes

Summer
Groundwater level
100-300 cm

Autumn
Groundwater level
80-200 cm

Winter
Groundwater level
5-120 cm

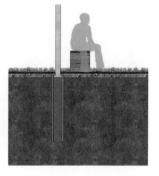

151 *Illustration of groundwater-driven windscreen pillars*

Wind Energy Bench

1. **General information** On many cool days, the wind comes from a typical direction, which can be different for different countries. This wind is uncomfortable and has to be blocked. Sitting on a bench can be much more comfortable on many days if the bench has windscreens on its sides. On cold days, however, this is not sufficient and you have to add an extra source of warmth. Such a heat generator can be a small wind turbine at the bottom of the bench. This turbine generates electricity converted into heat to warm up the bench.

2. **Effectiveness** The combination of the heated bench and the wind protection makes this a very effective solution.

3. **Extra advantages** The small wind turbine can visualize the wind speed at street level in an interesting manner. For children, it can be an educational object that teaches them about wind in the urban environment.

4. **Disadvantages** The bench has to be placed in well-ventilated places; otherwise it won't work.

5. **Construction** The planning and construction is work for specialists, as is the installation.

6. **Maintenance** The bench itself requires normal upkeep (e.g. painting). Specialists have to maintain the wind turbine frequently.

7. **Costs** € €

8. **No regret:** Yes

152 *Illustration of the wind energy bench*

Warm Windscreen Bench

1. **General information** Combining wind protection and warming a sitting person through longwave emission can generate an especially warm place. Think of a bench with a very large, stone back, placed at right angles to the prevailing wind, and thus offering good wind protection in many situations. The stone back receives and stores much shortwave radiation and emits it as warmth from the afternoon.

2. **Effectiveness** The back offers very good wind protection. If the sun does not shine, the bench absorbs less radiation and also emits less longwave radiation. So the effectiveness of the longwave radiation depends on the incoming radiation that was absorbed earlier.

3. **Extra advantages** Besides improving the microclimate, the large back can also be specially designed as public art and have aesthetic value.

4. **Disadvantages** The bench is less effective when the wind comes from a different direction and on cloudy days.

5. **Construction** The construction is not too complicated. Professionals can do it, but experienced laypeople can do it as well.

6. **Maintenance** The maintenance is minimal.

7. **Costs** €

8. **No regret:** No

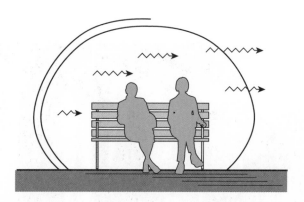

153 *Illustration of a warm windscreen bench*

208

Designing for Psychological Aspects of Microclimate Experience

Influencing 'Ambiance' Through Spatial Configuration

The fact that people very consciously perceive wide, open spaces as uncomfortable (and thus try to avoid these), plus the fact that the microclimate often is indeed problematic, often requires intervention. When urban outdoor spaces have to be made more suitable for dwelling there, you have to adjust the spatial proportions and openness. This can be done by placing buildings in different configurations, but also by adding larger vegetation elements such as trees (also see section 6.2). The openness of large spaces can be broken with many of the different elements discussed before for the manipulation of shadow and wind. This is not to say that a space should be filled with these elements. A few 'comfort islands' often do the trick. These can add to the required diversification of the microclimate. People often do have a clear preference for green elements. When you make spaces smaller or place elements that change the microclimate, your design obviously has to factor in other functions. On market squares, for example, there has to be sufficient room for the stalls and logistics. Terrains for events have to have open spaces for attractions and tents and such; and parks have to provide room for people to play and exercise.

154 *'Comfort island' with trees and palm trees on the Main Quad, Stanford University, USA*

Influencing 'Ambiance' through Materials

The materials used in urban spaces also influence the temperature experience – partly in line with the measurable facts and partly less so (also see section 2.3). In this context, especially the use of 'warm' materials such as wood, sandstone and bricks is recommended. We do have to keep in mind that many of these materials store quite a lot of heat and increase the urban heat island effect. It is therefore better to make a well-balanced use of these materials and apply them in strategically important places, for instance places where many people see the materials. It is also better to avoid using materials with a cold appearance (steel, glass, concrete, marble, enamel, tiles) in outdoor spaces. This last recommendation does not apply to areas with many people originating from for instance the Middle East or Southern Europe, where these materials invoke a 'feeling' of thermal comfort.

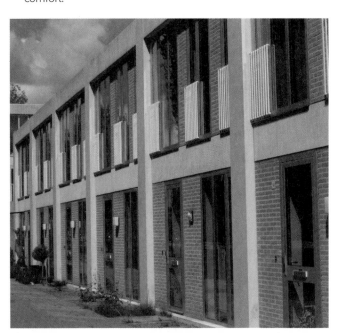

155 *A 'warm', light combination of materials in Rotterdam, the Netherlands*

Influencing 'Ambiance' through Colours

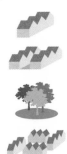

Colours also have a big influence on the experience of 'cold' and 'warm' spaces. As indicated before, colour only has a limited physical effect on the temperature. That is why applying colours is a suitable way to invoke cool or warm microclimate associations. Changing the colours, for example by painting facades in a different colour, is often a relatively easy and inexpensive intervention to change the ambiance. You have to keep in mind, though, that manipulative use of colour is a very simple solution. Because the actual physical problem (like heat or wind) is not addressed, we have to see this as treatment of the symptoms, not as a structural solution. We also have to keep in mind that people from different cultural backgrounds have different associations with colours. The use of colours could address these associations.

156 *Light and 'warm' colour combination in apartment facades in Vienna, Austria*

7

The Future of Urban Climate Responsive Design

In this book, I've written about how special the weather in the city is and that cities have their own climates. Climate change will add to the warming of the urban climate in our cities in the temperate zone. This will intensify the problems with urban heat we already have. The climate affects the lives of many people living in cities. I have therefore described the influence the urban climate directly has on people. For this, I have used the concept of 'microclimate experience'. The microclimate experience primarily entails the experience of temperature, wind and ambiance. Urban design can be of influence on all these factors.

But before people start implementing design interventions, the urban climate has to be analysed at the scale of those interventions. This is very important, because the urban climate is different everywhere, depending on the city's location, the configuration of districts and open areas, of streets and buildings. The analyses and design interventions can be made for different scale levels. Generally speaking, air temperature and ventilation can be influenced on the larger scale; and sun and shadow, wind protection and ambiance on a small-scale level. For all scale levels, this book offers many different solutions for influencing the urban climate. As you can see, many of these interventions aren't only good for the microclimate, but also for other important themes such as biodiversity, rain water storage, energy conservation and aesthetic value. Therefore integral designs are needed with climatological *and* other themes in mind.

I hope this book has shown that the urban climate is a fascinating combination of invisible processes around us, characterized by radiation, heat and dynamics. You will look at the city with new eyes! All these volatile and invisible processes are clear to you now. You don't only feel them, but can 'see' them as well. With this knowledge, you can analyse many aspects of the urban climate yourself, without having to involve experts such as meteorologists. Making these analyses isn't just necessary, but exciting too, since it brings new insights and interesting challenges to address with solutions. And finally, you can also start influencing the urban climate with the knowledge you've gained from this book. You have seen that we can largely design the urban climate, and that there are numerous possibilities to do so. Because the interactions within the urban climate are unique for each location, every design for the urban climate is unique for each location as well. Even though there are many 'ephemeral' interactions in the urban climate, using urban climate responsive design can offer a 'common thread' in design processes. As the landscape architect Mathieu Derckx once said during a workshop on urban climate responsive design: 'The theme urban climate gives you something to hold on to. You can base designs on it and rationalize them with it.' I hope this book conveyed how exciting, inspirational and sometimes very innovative designing with the urban climate can be!

We are already facing problems with the urban climate now and these will only get worse in the future. So we should act now and adapt our cities to these problems. And everyone can make a contribution.

The government sector has much influence. Policymakers and cities can incorporate urban climate adaptation in their decision making, and make it part of their urban master plans and other large-scale plans. Municipal civil servants that co-design the structure of the city can incorporate urban climate adaptation in zoning schemes, embed it in design ordinances or building regulations, or take it up in guidelines for public space planning. In countries where the planning system does not offer such tools, they can still do a lot. This entails raising public awareness, stimulating bottom-up initiatives and creating incentives for house owners, housing and retail corporations.

Landscape architects, urban designers and designers of public space working for design companies can also do much to foster implementation of adaptation measures. If the urban climate is a constant theme in their designs, it will naturally be part of the design of the city. Designing for the urban climate forms a new specialism for this group, which can bring in new commissions. Designers can also have a very important role as 'visualizers'. They can show how different our cities would look if they were adapted to the circumstances of the urban climate. Over the past few years, I have experienced the power of visualizations through my consulting work. I have worked often and intensively with municipalities and citizens on urban climate adaptation and have used visualizations frequently. Our designs and visualizations were always met with much enthusiasm, because they made the 'invisible' theme of the urban climate tangible. So there is a potentially new field of work for many spatial designers here. And in economically uncertain times it can be a good investment to specialize yourself in this future-oriented theme of urban climate adaptation.

157 *The alderman unveils the world's first 'urban climate tree' in Arnhem*

All the other people who also 'make the city', such as the catering industry and retail managers, shopkeepers' associations, neighbourhood councils and other interest groups, can also contribute by demanding urban climate adaptation measures from municipalities, designers and private owners. But these private owners can also start with urban climate adaptation in their own houses and gardens or their immediate urban environment. For instance, citizens of the city of Arnhem and I have planted the world's first 'urban climate tree' – a tree on a bare square in their 'overheated' urban district. This tree has an ornate ring that indicates the role of trees in improving the urban climate. This way, the citizens have not only improved the urban climate in their own neighbourhood, but they have also made a statement to raise awareness for urban climate – a world first!

Last but not least, all future 'makers' of the city should of course also know something about the urban climate and its adaptation. All students in landscape architecture, urban design, public space, design, city management and planning should be educated in this. To this end, the urban climate theme should be part of the curricula of many universities and universities of applied sciences. I am in the lucky position to have participated – and continue to do so – in the development of courses for students and professionals for such institutions. But now we need to start training more new 'educators' for this topic in order to meet the growing interest for courses on urban climate adaptation.

It is my hope that this book helps all these people and institutions involved to make concrete steps in urban climate adaptation. To share all this knowledge about the urban climate in a practical and personal way, I will happily keep giving lectures, seminars and design workshops. My dream is to form a *community of practice* with you, dear readers, in which we can work on improving the urban climate together and thus create comfortable cities!

158 *Professionals enthusiastically designing for urban climate at a workshop*

Index

Recommended Literature

Bottema, M., 'Wind climate and urban geometry', Doctoral Thesis University of Eindhoven (Helmond: Wibro, 1993)

Boutet, T., *Controlling Air Movement: A Manual for Architects and Builders* (New York: McGraw-Hill ,1987)

Brown, R.D., *Design with Microclimate-The Secret to Comfortable Outdoor Space* (Washington D.C.: Island Press, 2010)

Brown, R.D. and Gillespie, T.J., *Microclimatic Landscape Design: Creating Thermal Comfort and Energy Efficiency* (New York: Wiley, 1995).

Erell, E., Pearlmutter, D., Williamson, T. J., *Urban Microclimate: Designing the Spaces Between Buildings* (Routledge, 2011)

Hebbert, M., Jankovic, V., Webb, B. (eds.), *City Weathers: Meteorology and Urban Design 1950-2010* (Manchester Architecture Research Centre, University of Manchester, 2011).

Hove, L.W. A. van, et al., 'Exploring The Urban Heat Island Intensity Of Dutch Cities', in: *City Weathers: Meteorology and Urban Design 1950-2010*, workshop, Manchester, UK, 23 - 24 June, 2011, Manchester Architecture Research Centre, University of Manchester, 2011)

Littlefair, P.J., *Environmental Site Layout Planning: Solar Access, Microclimate and Passive Cooling In Urban Areas* (London: CRC BRE Publications, 2000)

Ministry of Economy Baden-Württemberg, *Climate Booklet for Urban Development* (Stuttgart, 2008)

Oke, T.R., *Boundary Layer Climates* (London: Methuen, 1987)

Santamouris, M., *Energy And Climate in the Urban Built Environment* (Routledge, 2013)

Sullivan, C., *Garden And Climate: Old World Techniques for Landscape Design,* (New York: McGraw-Hill, 2002)

Photographs and Figures Used in this Book

Illustration 4 Higher mortality during the heat wave of 2003 in several European countries
(adapted from: Haines, A., Kovats, R. S., Campbell-Lendrum, D., Corvalan, C., 2006, *Climate Change and Human Health: Impacts, Vulnerability and Public Health*, Public health 120(7):585-596)

Illustration 7 Types of radiation in the atmosphere and at the earth's surface
(adapted from: https://www.google.nl/search?gs_rn=17&gs_ri=psy-ab&tok=Cc9cquaw2eHCx2_Fy1PPQw&suggest=p&cp=8&gs_id=u&xhr=t&q=straling&bav=on.2,or.r_qf.&bvm=bv.48175248,d.d2k&biw=1416&bih=729&wrapid=tljp1371720318649014&um=1&ie=UTF-8&hl=en&tbm=isch&source=og&sa=N&tab=wi&ei=gsrCUZ3alsaoowX-nYDYBA#um=1&hl=en&tbm=isch&sa=1&q=stralingsbalans&oq=stralingsbalans&gs_l=img.3..oi24.10645.11740.1.12033.6.2.0.4.4.0.145.241.1j1.2.0...0.0...1c.1.17.img.kdodQ1to65A&bav=on.2,or.r_qf.&fp=b45b5c14f8f948a2&biw=1416&bih=729&facrc=_&imgdii=_&imgrc=ojjhKmx798XZrM%3A%3B4tlYVWpZDqffcM%3Bhttp%253A%252F%252Fwww.klimaatwebsite.be%252Fklimaat%252FAT%252FPIX%252FWarmtebalans.jpg%3Bhttp%253A%252F%252Fwww.klimaatwebsite.be%252Fklimaat%252FMAP.php%253Fp%253DAT%252FAT_15%2526m%253DAT%252FM04%3B650%3B480)

Illustration 8 Different angles of the sun in different parts of the world
(adapted from: Kunne, D.; Floors, R.; Meijer, L.; Wolters, H.J.; Sijbers, J.; Elberse, J.; Hageman, S.; Linssen, G.; Drummen, M.; Vries, A. de; Klok, L.; Brandsma, T. *Summer in the City : weersverschijnselen en luchtkwaliteit in de stad,* Wageningen 2010, p. 16)

Illustration 10 List of albedo, emissivity and thermal conductivity of different materials
(compiled from: Brown, R. D., Gillespie, T. J., *Microclimatic Landscape Design : Creating Thermal Comfort and Energy Efficiency,* New York: Wiley, 1995; Littlefair, P. J., *Environmental Site Layout Planning: Solar Access, Microclimate and Passive Cooling in Urban Areas,* London: CRC BRE Publications, 2000, pp. VIII; Meyer, H., *Skript zum Vertiefungsblock "Klima in urbanen Räumen",* Freiburg: Universität Freiburg, 2002,)

Illustration 12 Infrared image of surface temperatures in the Dutch city of Rotterdam, clearly showing the heat archipelago
(gemeentewerken Rotterdam, *Kennis voor Klimaat rapport Hittestress in Rotterdam,* rapportnummer KvK/039/2011, Rotterdam, 2011)

Illustration 13 Wind rose for Detroit City Airport during the fall 2010 period
(Snyder, M., Arunachalam, S., , Isakov, V., Talgo K., Naess B, Valencia A., Omary M., Davis N., Cook R., Hanna, A., 2014 *'Creating Locally-Resolved Mobile-Source Emissions Inputs for Air Quality Modeling in Support of an Exposure Study in Detroit'* Int. J. Environ. Res. Public Health 2014, 11(12), Figure 4)

Illustration 15 Valley wind systems during the day and at night
(adapted from: Liljequist, G.H., *Allgemeine Meteorologie,* Braunschweig: Friedrich Vieweg Verlag,1994)

Illustration 17 Profile of large-scale wind over open landscapes, woods or sparsely built-up areas and densely built-up cities
(adapted from: Bjerregaard, E. , Nielsen, F. *Vindmiljø omkring bygninger,* SBI Anvisning 128, Statens Byggeforskningsinstitut, 1981,)

Illustration 18 In a wind tunnel, fine dust is blown around a building volume to see how the wind flows
(source unknown)

Illustration 19 Wind flows around a shelterbelt
(adapted from: Oke, T. R., *Boundary Layer Climates,* London: Methuen, 1987, pp. 435., p. 245)

Illustration 20 Wind profiles for different types of groves
(adapted from: Robinette, G. O., MacClennon, C., *Landscape Planning for Energy Conservation,* New York: Van Nostrand Reinhold, 1983, pp. 224., p. 35)

Illustrations 21-25 Wind flows around buildings
(adapted from: Blocken, B., Carmeliet, J., 2004, *Pedestrian Wind Environment Around Buildings: Literature Review and Practical Examples,* Journal of Thermal Envelope and Building Science 28(2):107-159.)

Illustration 26 Diagram with different building depths and the expected sheltered areas at their leeside
(adapted from: Boutet, T., *Controlling Air- movement,* New York: Mc Graw Hill, 1987, figure 6.8)

Illustration 30 Wind flows in a street
(Kim, J.-J., Baik, J.-J., 2004, *A Numerical Study of the Effects of Ambient Wind Direction on Flow and Dispersion in Urban Street Canyons Using the RNG k–E Turbulence Model,* Atmospheric Environment 38(19):3039-3048.

Illustration 31 Profiles of the three wind regimes: skimming flow, wake interference and isolated roughness flow (adapted from: Oke, T. R., *Boundary Layer Climates,* London: Methuen, 1987, p. 267)

Illustration 48 Infrared photographs showing the surface temperatures in Arnhem, the Netherlands (gemeente Arnhem, 2009)

Illustration 50 Example of simulations of valley winds in Freiburg, Germany (source unknown)

Illustration 51 Urban heat map of Hong Kong (Courtesy of Planning Department of the HKSAR Government. The map (2009) was made by Professor Edward Ng, Professor Ren Chao of the Chinese University of Hong Kong and Professor Lutz Katzschner of Kassel University (all rights reserved))

Illustration 52 Urban climate map of Arnhem, the Netherlands (gemeente Arnhem and Kassel University)

Illustration 62 Recommendations map Arnhem, the Netherlands (gemeente Arnhem)

Illustration 63 Analysis and recommendation maps for valley winds, forming a basis for zoning plans, Stuttgart, Germany (Landeshauptstadt Stuttgart, Referat Städtebau und Umwelt, Amt für Stadtplanung und Stadterneuerung, Abteilung Städtebauliche Planung Mitte, *Rahmenplan Halbhöhenlagen* 2008, figures 5.02 and 10.06)

Illustration 68 A model of a city in the wind tunnel (Peutz associés, Mook)

Illustration 69 Smoke simulations in the wind tunnel of Colorado State University (https://www.google.nl/search?hl=en&site=imghp&tbm=isch&s ource=hp&biw=1224&bih=618&q=wind+tunnel+colorado+state +university&oq=wind+tunnel+colorado+state+university&gs_l= img.12...953.19771.0.21091.68.22.13.33.39.1.188.2090.11j10.21.0....0...1 ac.1.26.img..32.36.1908.ruvfNv8YtSE#facrc=_&imgrc=jiokKo9FJ3w DOM%3A%3BchzKofl9cSY61M%3Bhttp%253A%252F%252Fuplo ad.wikimedia.org%252Fwikipedia%252Fcommons%252F4%252 F4d%252FEXPERIMENTAL_WIND_TUNNEL_DEVICE_BUILT_AT_ COLORADO_STATE_UNIVERSITY._SMOKE_IS_PIPED_INTO_THIS_ MODEL_OF_THE_CITY_OF..._-_NARA_-_543752.jpg%3Bhttp%253A %252F%252Fcommons.wikimedia.org%252Fwiki%252FFile%253A EXPERIMENTAL_WIND_TUNNEL_DEVICE_BUILT_AT_COLORADO_ STATE_UNIVERSITY._SMOKE_IS_PIPED_INTO_THIS_MODEL_OF_ THE_CITY_OF..._-_NARA_-_543752.jpg%3B3000%3B2027)

Illustration 70 CFD-wind simulations for a project in The Hague, the Netherlands (Peutz associés, Mook)

Illustration 73 Measurement transects in Toronto with differences in air temperature (red) and solar radiation (blue) (Graham Slater)

Illustration 77 Observations maps of stationary presence in Kassel, Germany Katzschner, L. , Bosch, U. , Röttgen, R., 2002, *Behaviour of People in Open Spaces in Dependency of Thermal Comfort Conditions*, Design with the environment, Proceedings of the 19th International Conference PLEA, Toulouse-France, 22nd - 24th July 2002, 411-415.)

Illustration 94 List of shadow depths of trees (Brown, R.D. and Gillespie, T.J., *Microclimatic Landscape Design : Creating Thermal Comfort and Energy Efficiency,* New York: Wiley, 1995, p. 116)

Illustration 95 List of trees and how 'climate proof' they are (translated from: http://www.umwelt.nrw.de/umwelt/pdf/ klimawandel/handbuch_stadtklima/kapitel4_S155-228.pdf, pag. 17 and 18)

Illustration 124 A mist shower in a shopping mall in California, USA (Marisa van den Berg)

Illustration 127 Street sprinklers in Lyon, France (http://blogs.grandlyon.com/plan-climat/2012/12/19/ilots-de-chaleur-la-buire-teste-le-rafraichissement-urbain/)

Illustration 131 Densities of windbreaks and the sheltered effect behind them (adapted from: Oke, T. R., *Boundary layer climates*, London: Methuen, 1987, p. 244)

Illustration 132 Windbreaks with different boarding and their effect on the wind patterns behind them (adapted from: Boutet, T., *Controlling Air Movement*, New York: Mc Graw Hill, 1987, pp. 79-81)

Illustration 133 Windbreaks of different heights, and angles and their wind speed reductions (Dierickx, W., Gabriels, D., Cornelis, W. M., 2002, *Wind Tunnel Study on Oblique Windscreens*, Biosystems Engineering 82(1):87-95.)

Illustration 145 Pergola with waterfall (Yi Shan)

Illustration 151 Illustration of groundwater-driven windscreen pillars (Darius Reznek)

Illustration 152 Illustration of the wind energy bench (Josje Hoefsloot)

Illustration 157 The alderman unveils the world's first 'urban climate tree' in Arnhem (Courtesy of Han Koppers)

Photos on introduction pages of chapters
3 Stock Exchange
4 Jorg Hackemann, Shutterstock.com
5 Shutterstock.com

All other photographs and illustrations: Sanda Lenzholzer and Landscape Architecture group, Wageningen University

Credits

Texts: Sanda Lenzholzer
Translation: Jean Tee
Copy editing: Leo Reijnen
Design: Ad van der Kouwe (Manifesta)
Cover photo: Tom Croes
Lithography and Printing: Koninklijke van Gorcum BV
Publisher: Marcel Witvoet, nai010 publishers

This publication was made possible by financial support from
Wageningen University and NHBOS Foundation.

nai010 publishers is an internationally orientated publisher specialized in developing,
producing and distributing books in the fields of architecture, urbanism, art and
design. www.nai010.com

nai010 books are available internationally at selected bookstores and from the
following distribution partners:

North, Central and South America - Artbook | D.A.P., New York,
USA, dap@dapinc.com

Rest of the world - Idea Books, Amsterdam, the Netherlands, idea@ideabooks.nl

For general questions, please contact nai010 publishers directly at sales@nai010.com
or visit our website www.nai010.com for further information.

Printed and bound in the Netherlands

ISBN 978-94-6208-198-7